In Bed with Strangers

In Bed with Strangers
Swinging My Way to Self-Discovery

Casey Donatello

Exposit

Jefferson, North Carolina

LIBRARY OF CONGRESS CATALOGUING-IN-PUBLICATION DATA

Names: Donatello, Casey, 1982– author.
Title: In bed with strangers : swinging my way to
self-discovery / Casey Donatello.
Description: Jefferson, NC : Exposit Books, [2018]
Identifiers: LCCN 2018015679 | ISBN 9781476675763
(softcover : acid free paper) ∞
Subjects: LCSH: Group sex.
Classification: LCC HQ23 .D576 2018 | DDC 306.77/3—dc23
LC record available at https://lccn.loc.gov/2018015679

BRITISH LIBRARY CATALOGUING DATA ARE AVAILABLE

**ISBN (print) 978-1-4766-7576-3
ISBN (ebook) 978-1-4766-3458-6**

© 2018 Casey Donatello. All rights reserved

*No part of this book may be reproduced or transmitted in any form
or by any means, electronic or mechanical, including photocopying
or recording, or by any information storage and retrieval system,
without permission in writing from the publisher.*

Front cover image © 2018 Alanpoulson/Dreamstime

Printed in the United States of America

Exposit is an imprint of McFarland & Company, Inc., Publishers

Box 611, Jefferson, North Carolina 28640
www.expositbooks.com

To anyone I have ever had sex with.
Whether good or bad, you made
an unforgettable impression on me.

Acknowledgments

Thank you to my coach who inspired me to dream outside the box.

A huge thank you to my publisher for taking a risk on me.

Thank you to Marcy and Amy for their acceptance and support regarding my life decisions and their invaluable assistance with the book.

Thank you to Max and Billy for your solid friendship.

And a special thanks to Luis for unleashing my wild side and continuously making my fantasies a reality.

Table of Contents

Acknowledgments   vi
Preface   1

1. Obedient Girl   3
2. Me   15
3. Butterfly   20
4. Sex-planations   26
5. Split Personality   38
6. Me versus We   44
7. A Different Flavor   55
8. Swinging Systems   63
9. Grin and Bare It   74
10. My Swinging BFF   80
11. Psycho Swinger   83
12. Socks and Soup   94
13. Triangular Fun   108
14. Extra M's   123
15. Limo Luis   126
16. Scarlet Fever   139
17. Reset   142
18. Resurrection   146

19. A Potential Peter	159
20. Out of My Shell	165
21. Red Hot	168
Epilogue	175
Extra info	177

Preface

Shame, self-doubt, love, loss, acceptance and survival are universal emotions. Everyone can relate to them regardless of the context. It took me more than a decade of living a double life to find happiness.

I am a 35-year-old white girl from the Upper East Side. I like the beach, yoga, salsa dancing, foreign movies and dinners with my girlfriends. I am average height and weight and I have brown hair and eyes. I do not normally stand out in a crowd. If you stood behind me at the deli counter or sat beside me on the train, you would hardly notice me. I could be your sister, your daughter, your co-worker, your friend. I am the girl next door.

If I told you I spent most of my free time fucking strangers from the Internet, what would your initial reaction be? Would you assume I was a trashy girl with no self-respect who used her body for attention and pity me? Or would you think I was living the ultimate fantasy of sexual freedom and envy me?

Would you have preconceived notions about my social status or family history? I'm sure most people would be surprised to know that I grew up in a typical upper-middle-class neighborhood, raised by conservative Catholic parents to regard sex as private and sacred.

So how does a seemingly ordinary and shy girl end up involved in a world filled with orgies and gang bangs? Was I spiraling out of control, going down a dark, destructive path? Or was I discovering a world of acceptance and happiness?

I'd like to think I am just a strong, independent woman following her own course. I am a modern-day swinger.

A Note to the Reader

Due to the sensitive nature of this book, I have changed the names and all identifying features of the people involved to respect their privacy. These superficial adjustments have no impact on the events or interactions that took place or the effect they had on me. This book is a true account of my experiences as I remember them.

(If you think you may recognize someone in this book, I kindly ask you to refrain from publicly acknowledging it. This book is meant to reveal *my* secret—not anyone else's. I will never confirm your suspicions.)

Chapter 1

Obedient Girl

Two thousand and four. I was 22; he was 38. He was the love of my life and my boss—my married boss. He was my sexual awakening. Before I met him, I was very inexperienced. I lost my virginity at 19 to my high school boyfriend. It was unceremonious and not nearly as magical as I anticipated. It was a Thursday night in August. There were no fireworks and no candles, just some vaginal discomfort. It left me dumbfounded as to all the hype about sex. Throughout our relationship I was a victim of chronic UTIs and irritation because, unbeknownst to me, I was allergic to latex.

I was self-conscious and timid around guys. I worried about what people thought about me. I feared I was not good enough. If a guy didn't call me back I was crippled with insecurity. I was forlorn, desperate for approval and affection. I required liquid courage to disguise my anxieties and loosened up a little after a few drinks. I was a big fan of making out and didn't mind if a boy felt my boobs under my shirt, but the pressure of having to give a good blow job when I didn't know how was too burdensome, so I just avoided it. The older I got the more terrifying it became because of my lack of experience. I didn't want to make a fool of myself if I got naked and had no clue what to do. What if I was terrible at sucking dick? What if I couldn't figure out how to move my body properly in unfamiliar positions? What if he came in my mouth and I was so disgusted I threw up? I was too embarrassed even to discuss sex with my girlfriends. Meeting Elliot changed *everything*.

My first job after graduating culinary school taught me more than how to cook. It was in a tiny, upscale French bistro in a trendy neighborhood in Brooklyn. Elliot was the general manager of the restaurant and I stumbled upon him during my tour of the kitchen. The minute I laid eyes on him, he had a magnetic hold on me. It sounds cliché, but our meeting was serendipitous.

He was engaged in a heated discussion with the executive chef about the new menu. Elliot was British, five feet, ten inches tall, had dark hair and a slim physique, and was clean-shaven and resembled Hugh Jackman. He radiated equanimity with his military-like posture and impeccably tailored pinstriped suit. The woman from HR escorting me interrupted them to introduce the latest hire. Elliot shook my hand and lingered an extra moment. Something transferred between us and there was no turning back.

Elliot enjoyed hanging out in the kitchen and hassling the cooks, playing pranks on them. He had a never-ending supply of jokes and his laugh was loud and infectious. He would stare at me from across the kitchen and found excuses to engage in conversation with me. He had recently quit smoking and always kept a toothpick between his lips. He had a taste for colorful bowties and shiny cufflinks. He was a die-hard Yankees fan and idolized Cary Grant. He would brush against me when he walked by and always offered to make me an espresso. His sarcastic sense of humor and cleverly insulting responses to people who pissed him off were brilliant. I admired the way he didn't take shit from anyone.

There had always been a level of tension between us, but he was married, so I never expected anything beyond innocent flirting to develop. I was raised to respect the value of marriage, and as a little girl, I never envisioned being a mistress. I was not a homewrecker. Only terrible people did things like that!

The staff routinely went out for drinks to a local bar after work so one night I went along. I socialized with several people but really wanted to talk to Elliot. I noticed him furtively watching me and I became intrigued. He walked over and joined the conversation I was having with another cook. He offered to buy me a drink, so we maneuvered through the crowd to the back bar together.

Out of sight of our coworkers, we were finally able to interact more personally. He sat close to me on a couch against the back wall and we talked as we sipped our beers. He asked about my education and how I liked the job so far, always staring at me like he was trying to read my mind. Often, I looked away because it made me nervous. As he

Chapter 1. Obedient Girl

moved closer, I sensed something was on the verge of happening. His hand moved from the arm of the couch to my thigh. I did not remove it. He leaned closer as he talked until his face was inches from mine. His hand moved to my lower back. Then he kissed me. He apologized, saying he couldn't resist. I froze. Then he kissed me again and I kissed him back. With that kiss, we officially crossed the line from employer/employee to lovers.

Elliot never wore a wedding ring and swore he only stayed with his wife for the sake of his six-year-old identical twin girls. He also couldn't afford to leave because paying for the house and school plus renting his own apartment was too expensive. I knew what we were doing was wrong. I always believed cheating was unacceptable, but I convinced myself our situation was an exception. His wife didn't understand him; she was no longer attracted to him. They hadn't had sex or even slept in the same bed for several years. Elliot was lonely and had needs. He seemed trapped and I wanted to be his savior. Elliot was the first man to make me feel important. He always told me he wished he had met me sooner and I was the perfect match for him. If he married her by mistake and was truly meant to be with me, then our relationship seemed more justifiable. It was fate's fault, not mine. I liked being needed. Fulfilling his desires gave me a purpose.

We tried to mask our torrid affair for our professional sakes, but it was impossible. We had sex in his office any chance we had. We locked the door and put towels at the bottom to block the light so anyone walking by would think it was unoccupied. After we fucked, he would exit first, then text me when the coast was clear so I could sneak out undetected. I returned to my station with flushed cheeks and a twinkle in my eye. Sometimes we fucked in his car in the parking lot after our shift ended. We gave our best effort to appear professional, but everyone could see right through us and soon the rumors spread like wildfire. Deny. Deny. Deny.

Dating a married man produced many side effects, shame and insecurity the biggest. Hiding his marital status created a lot of stress for me. I stopped hanging out with friends who asked too many questions. I didn't want to admit he was married, but I didn't want to lie about it, so I just avoided it. I distanced myself from family members who suspected something was wrong. I didn't mind losing my life to keep him.

He proclaimed he loved me so much he could live in a cardboard box with me and be happy. I truly believed we would end up together. I was so lovesick I even bought my own apartment just so we could have a place to hang out. A private love nest. It was going to be the solution to all our problems. He could move in with me and not have to pay rent. I would make our dreams come true. I thought it was that simple. Oh, how wrong I was!

We spent a lot of time together—when it was convenient for *him*. We spent all day working and all night hanging out. He would sleep at my place, tell his wife he was working late, and claim he needed to stay at a hotel because he was too tired to drive home. Whenever he answered a text, I wondered if he was replying to her. On his days off, I never saw him.

Occasionally I wondered what would happen if there was an emergency. What if he got into a fatal car crash or had a heart attack? How would I know? Who would tell me? Would I even go to his funeral? If we accidentally bumped into someone he knew while we were out in public, I was introduced as a coworker. The person might ask how his wife and kids were. It sent chills down my spine. I felt *invisible*. I felt *inadequate*.

He had to portray the part of the devoted father and husband. In the beginning, I was genuinely interested in his daughters. Who were their favorite princesses? What were their favorite subjects? Their favorite colors? Eventually I saw them as competition. My enemies. They were the reason Elliot couldn't be mine. How fucked up is that to say?! Logically, I understood they were innocent victims in this web of deceit. But as they got older they needed their father more. Dance recitals. Field trips. Birthday parties. Rightfully, they were higher priority than I was, but it didn't make the pain any more bearable. I began changing the topic when he mentioned them. Why should I discuss these kids I was never allowed to meet? They didn't even know I existed. I thought it was so selfish of Elliot to torture me like that. But when Elliot would complain how stressful and exhausting it was to maintain this fake persona, I would listen and take pity on him. How terrible it must be for him, pretending to be happy when he would rather be here with me. When he went on family vacations, I sat home and cried, consumed with jealousy and insecurity. I felt worthless. All the pain always disappeared when he returned to my arms and said he loved me. The good times made me forget the bad times, or at least excuse them. It is astounding what a person can convince herself of.

Elliot was uber sexual and kinky. He taught me how to understand my body and actually enjoy sex. Prior to him, I had a few sexual experiences that left me wondering why people loved sex so much. Sex had been so mechanical and boring. I'd suffer through it to satisfy my partner. I'd rush through it just to get it over with. Sex was basically a chore, my womanly duty. Elliot gave me my first orgasm and it was like a light bulb going off. An "'Aha!' moment," as Oprah would say. Oh, I should be getting pleasure from this in addition to giving it? Oh, the guy should not be the only one cumming? Oh, I should participate because I enjoy this and not because I feel obligated to do it? It was an epic revelation. Before Elliot, I had sex because that's what people do. After Elliot, I had sex because I *wanted* to.

Our relationship was fiery and passionate and being with him was like the greatest high. The excitement of a roller coaster climbing up the tracks and the adrenaline of it plummeting down the other side. We explored light bondage and rough sex. Elliot would tie my hands, choke me, pull my hair. The energy I felt from his pleasure made me feel alive.

He had a major foot fetish and admitted he fell for me the day he saw my bare heel while I was changing shoes. The idea of him being attracted to my feet seemed odd, but when I realized that humoring him benefited me, I decided to take it more seriously. He loved when I wore shoes with no socks. He couldn't wait to smell my feet as I rubbed them on his face. If I texted him a picture of my bare foot he would get instantly hard. Sometimes I jerked him off with my feet; other times he masturbated in my socks before I wore them. I got pedicures every week to keep my feet pristine. The power I had over him literally in a single toe. Foot fetishes are monumentally particular. The arousal can come from the shape or size of the toes, the feel of the sole, the curve of the arch, the smell from the material of the shoe, the style of the shoe, anything. Every foot fetishist has his own unique preferences. This was the first time I understood my body was a source of *power*.

After a while, we started exploring other avenues to take us to a new level—that's when we found swinging. Elliot wanted to see me with another woman. He wanted to watch us kiss and touch. He told me his wife was not willing to explore his sexual curiosities, so I immediately thought this was the perfect opportunity to prove I was the better woman for him. The old cliché "a woman in the street and a freak in the sheets" kept playing in my mind. That was the solution to keeping my man happy. I wasn't sure if I liked girls—I honestly had never thought about it—but I wanted to make his fantasy a reality.

Elliot was working late while I was home searching the casual encounters section on Craigslist, reading posts from other people looking for sex. Men seeking women, women seeking men, men and women looking for women, men and women looking for trannies. How fascinating that people do this! It sounded provocative but intriguing, disturbing yet exciting. So risqué. I viewed sex as something sacred between people in love, not a leisure activity among strangers.

Amid these posts, I came across an ad for an adult club—a swingers' club. I wasn't exactly sure what that meant so I curiously clicked on the link. Friday night was for couples and single men, but Saturday was couples only. It was "on premise" meaning sex was allowed, the event was BYOB, and you had to RSVP to attend. I couldn't comprehend this was a legitimate thing. How could you be allowed to have sex at a club? My interest was piqued so I called Elliot and told him I wanted to go. He was shocked but thrilled with his obedient princess. The adventure would change my life forever.

Around 10 the following Saturday night, we drove straight from work to the club and I changed in the car. I felt nervous and anxious. I was not prepared for what was ahead and I had no idea what to expect. We were inexperienced and uneducated about this world. Until a few days earlier, I hadn't even known it existed. What kind of people would be there? Were they weird? Would we fit in? Would I enjoy the experience or regret it? Would this be enough to cause Elliot to leave his boring and inadequate marriage?

Elliot turned down a dark side street and into a busy parking lot. A young valet wearing a black vest approached us and escorted us to the front door of a large, non-descript building. Then suddenly I was in a tight little black dress, holding my boyfriend's hand, in the middle of a room filled with naked people. I was in awe. Lockers for personal belongings and unnecessary clothes lined the left wall. The check-in counter and coat check were to the right. Elliot gave our names and

Chapter 1. Obedient Girl

paid the entrance fee. Beyond that was a bar and a dance floor with a DJ. It was visual overload for my brain. I didn't know where to look or what to do. A sex swing hung in one corner and other sex contraptions that I was unfamiliar with were stationed around it. Porn was blasting on several TV screens in multiple areas. One channel showed a young blond girl with way too much makeup getting anally fucked by a black dude while she moaned unrealistically. Another station had a redhead and a brunette taking turns sucking a muscular guy's dick.

Baskets of condoms and lube were scattered near every couch and table. The sandwich platters and bowls of chips on a buffet table against the back wall was humorous to me. Who came here to eat? People casually mingled at the bar, totally naked, with no compunction. It was as if they didn't notice they were naked. A flirty brunette bartender made drinks. Euphoric screams reverberated from the orgy taking place a few feet away. Crowds gathered around to watch. The atmosphere mesmerized us.

We peeked upstairs and found a small smoking lounge with two couches and a coffee table. Toilets, showers and towels were available for those who wanted to clean up afterward. Back downstairs, we strolled through the public sex areas, which consisted of several large mattresses on the floor in one large open area. A hallway lined with private rooms where couples could close the door and regulate who entered was guarded by a large bouncer sitting on a stool. Other staff roamed the floor to ensure safety.

The crowd was mostly middle-aged and very friendly. Patrons welcomed us with smiles and asked if we had been there before and how long we had been in the Lifestyle. How did we hear about the club and whose idea was it to come? First timers, we replied. Some of the people we met were also novices, while others had been frequenting the club for years. The vibe was inviting and comfortable.

Elliot and I familiarized ourselves with the space and just observed how other people interacted. Several couples were piled on one bed, bodies tangled. A man was sitting on a couch with his pants around his ankles while a woman knelt before him sucking his dick. Two drunk topless girls kissed as they fondled each other on the dance floor as their men watched.

One girl caught my interest. Tamara had a few extra pounds but a beautiful, innocent face and long, dark wavy hair. She had a Gothic look, wearing a black leather skirt and black corset and thick black eyeliner and bright pink lipstick. Something about her attracted me. Maybe it eased my nerves because I was slimmer and prettier than she was. It made her less threatening. Elliot struck up a conversation with her while I sipped a drink at the bar. He learned that she was with her husband but allowed to party alone.

With his permission, we ushered her to a private room, which was more like a closet with a twin mattress on the floor. There was barely enough room to stand on the floor and not touch the mattress. It was far from luxurious. Elliot closed the door and it was hot, no air circulation at all. Elliot became the director. Tamara was submissive and he told her to kiss me. It was surreal, almost like a dream. I couldn't fathom this was really happening. How did I, this introverted girl, end up in a sex club with a naked girl on top of me? As we gently kissed, I ran my fingers through her hair, then traced the curves of her body with my fingertips. I marveled at her soft skin and her floral-smelling hair. I panted heavily as her mouth moved to my neck then my chest. She nibbled on my hard nipples and my entire body tingled. Tamara's mouth journeyed lower to my belly button. Then she went down on me. The sensation was incredible. Her warm tongue between my legs drove me crazy. I closed my eyes and moaned.

Tamara obeyed Elliot's command to treat me roughly. He ordered her to bite me and pull my hair. It was erotic to see him watching us with immense pleasure. I felt like a porn star. I felt sexy and naughty. I felt like the complete opposite of my normal self and that was the most invigorating part. When the show was over Tamara was excused and Elliot and I fucked with a level of passion I had never experienced.

The next day I went to work as if it never happened. I would occasionally snicker to myself as I thought about it. Elliot sent me several texts telling me how turned on he was and how he couldn't wait to do it again. We now shared this secret. The connection between us was stronger than ever.

Elliot and I became regulars at the club. It was our unspoken routine. Every Saturday we hit the sex club. The owner knew us by name and always shook Elliot's hand and hugged me when he saw us. Sometimes we only had sex with each other; sometimes we hooked up with

Chapter 1. Obedient Girl

other people. We had explored other clubs but found this to be the most laid-back crowd and comfortable, open space. I grew to feel so at home the minute we walked in I would strip down to my bra and panties. I liked the freedom. Like Eve in the Garden of Eden before all the shit hit the fan. Flaunting my body and receiving attention from the other members delighted me. Seeing women who were heavier, older and less attractive confidently parading around naked allowed me to feel better about myself. I admired their bravery. If they could be confident, why couldn't I? My body was young and perky and this was the place I could strut it. Elliot loved showing me off. He got a thrill knowing the other men there were drooling over me. I was proud that he was proud to be there with me.

After a few more girl-girl episodes, we graduated to the next phase, soft swap (trading partners for oral sex but no intercourse). Elliot was much more social and forward than I was. Even with my growing confidence, I still preferred him to do the dirty work. I would point out candidates I found acceptable and Elliot would make the initial contact and set it up. If a couple propositioned us but I wasn't interested, I made Elliot decline them. I enjoyed the experiences, but I still relied on Elliot for security and permission to act out our fantasies. My main goal was to turn him on.

Our first soft swap was with a fairly experienced couple. Elliot and I were at the bar drinking a beer and the couple had been sitting at a table a few feet away from us. I noticed them stare occasionally. I made eye contact, which coaxed them to walk over and introduce themselves. Sarah was in her mid-30s and skinny, had shoulder-length dirty blond hair, and was wearing a white blouse, a super short plaid skirt and black heels. She looked like a slutty schoolgirl. Rich was in his early 40s, had a close buzz-cut, and was wearing a black button-down dress shirt and jeans. As typical pick-up lines go, they inquired about how long we had been in the Lifestyle, how often we came here and whose idea it had been to try swinging. We answered and politely asked about them. They had been married ten years, swinging for two. We casually talked over another drink and then Rich asked if we would be interested in going somewhere quieter. Elliot looked at me and I said, "Sure, why not?"

The four of us wandered around the club, checking what activities were taking place in the public rooms, and continued down the hall to the private rooms. All the doors were closed, so we just hung out and continued talking while we waited for a vacancy. As we talked I leaned against Elliot with my head resting on his arm. This was new territory. I was curious how this would play out. I planned to follow Elliot's lead as usual.

A door opened and two couples exited. Their faces were flushed, and their clothes disheveled, but they were all smiling. They nodded to us as they walked by as if to silently say, "Your turn, have fun." The bouncer asked us to be patient as he changed the sheets and tidied up the room. Cleanliness was always a priority.

This room was slightly larger than ones we had been in before with a full-size mattress jammed into it. It was awkward at first because I didn't know what the procedure was. How did this start? Rich motioned for us to sit down on the bed and get comfortable. I obliged and Sarah sat on my left side and Elliot on my right. Rich was next to Sarah. The room got very quiet. I snuggled close to Elliot. Rich broke the ice and said, "Sarah, isn't she beautiful?" Sarah agreed. Rich said, "Wouldn't you like to kiss her?" Again, Sarah agreed. She leaned in and pressed her lips against mine. As we kissed, I felt her hand move up my leg, across my stomach and over my breasts. Her intentions became more focused. She kissed me harder, touched me more intimately. I felt the weight on the mattress shift as Elliot and Rich moved away to give us space. Without Elliot's body for support mine slowly lowered as Sarah wrapped her arms around me. I was horizontal with her on top of me.

She lifted my shirt and pushed my bra down to expose my tits. She sucked on them while I played with her hair. Rich said, "Elliot, isn't this a lovely sight?" Hearing Elliot agree gave me a little boost. I wanted to turn him on, so I became more proactive, kissing and touching Sarah. The energy between us increased and she lifted my skirt. She teasingly kissed me over my panties. I felt another hand on my thigh, and when I looked, I saw Rich joining in. He was rubbing his cock through his jeans as he touched me. Elliot sat down next to me and kissed me as Sarah ate my pussy. Things were heating up now. Rich removed his hand from himself and used it to finger Sarah as she moaned, her mouth full of my pussy.

When Sarah was done, she sat up and moved over so Rich could get a taste. Elliot and Sarah began kissing and she unbuckled his belt and started blowing him. It was a bizarre sight to see another girl on your boyfriend's dick. I wasn't sure how I felt. Was I jealous or turned on? There was a signal delay between my eyes and my brain. I didn't have a chance to contemplate it because Rich was giving me an orgasm.

The four of us mingled a little longer and then we fucked our own partners. Sarah and I were on all fours facing each other. We held hands and randomly kissed while our men fucked us until they came. When we were done, it was a little weird thanking each other and bidding each other adieu as we sorted out who this thong or that sock belonged to.

Elliot and I headed back to the bar for another beer. We stayed a little longer to unwind after the excitement. When we got home we fucked again as we relived the night. That was the sexiest part—having sex and thinking about what we just did.

The next step would have been full swap, but I was not comfortable having sex with other people. I wasn't secure enough and was a little bitter thinking about it. Already struggling with the fact that Elliot was married, I needed to keep something for myself. If he could fuck any woman he wanted, then why would he need me? How could I give him what he wanted but retain a little ownership?

We lived this life for several years and even joined a site online to meet other swingers. Occasionally we would meet couples for drinks or dinner and then fuck around. Looking back, we were not a strong enough couple to truly embrace this. We had a lot of our own issues and broke up eventually, but not because of swinging.

I turned 30 and the bubble burst. I resented Elliot for never leaving his wife. I hated him for the excuses. I despised him for wasting my time. I felt used for his sexual appetite. I felt robbed of the years I dedicated to a doomed relationship. What if I missed out on meeting the real man of my dreams because I loved a man who deceived me for so long? The best years of my life, my 20s, were gone.

Elliot did not want to let me go. Why would he? He got everything he wanted from me. He had an extremely volatile temper and he fought dirty. He called me a slut and a whore when he wanted to undermine me. He was a master at making me feel guilty. Like I did something wrong. Like I was selfish for demanding he get divorced. Like I was unfair for not wanting to be his secret lover. His manipulating arguments sounded so heartfelt that I kept giving him more chances. Our breakup lasted about a year. I thought I would never be free. Years later I found out he never left his wife. It validated my choice to leave him.

Chapter 2

Me

In my mid–30s, I can finally say that I am content. If my deviant sexual preferences shock you, guess what? They shock me even more. In the beginning, whenever I found myself naked on a bed in a hotel room with someone I just met a few minutes earlier, I'd ask myself, "What the hell is wrong with you? Why can't you just be normal? What would people think if they knew?" I mean, seriously. Adding "swinger" to my resume was never my goal. I randomly stumbled into it. I am a diffident girl with social anxiety, yet somehow I have the ability to morph into a bold, courageous, ferocious female when it comes to interacting with anonymous sexual partners. It has been a long, bewildering, emotional, stressful journey but I have finally come to realize that I am simply not meant to have a so-called normal life. I am unconventional.

Although I had no fucking clue what my destiny was, I was sure of one thing from an early age—marriage and kids were not in my future. They never appealed to me. It sounds terrible, but I perceived having kids as a life-ending event. A prison sentence. I only saw the negative effects of it, not the beauty. I'm not sure why, but trust me, I felt guilty about it. Maybe deep down I feared being a parent because it was permanent. I couldn't run away if things got too tough. Besides, how could I raise a stable child when I was always hanging on by a thread?

I was always fielding questions about my personal life. I felt like an outcast for my choice, as if being single was a contagious disease. As if I was less of a person because I didn't have a doting husband, adorable children and a white picket fence. I was endlessly justifying myself, swearing I was fine without a man. If I could only be honest and tell anyone who questioned me "Hey, I am having more sex in one month than you have in a year or a lifetime," maybe I would be left alone. But

I couldn't. Sex is taboo still—especially the kind I have—so I felt forced to veil my true identity, which was a constant struggle.

I am not trying to boast or flaunt my sexual conduct, but I can't write a book about sex without writing about sex. There is a reason for every story I tell. I just sincerely hope to make people understand that a person's sex life should not matter. I do not want to be persecuted for mine. Swinging opened my eyes to an alternative lifestyle where I felt embraced and I could be myself without fear of judgment. I have learned to be who I want to be and not who I think other people expect me to be. It is a colossal relief, so liberating. I have come such a long way from where I started.

I am plain. I wear yoga clothes and sneakers, sports bras and cotton underwear. Sometimes I don't even brush my hair and I rarely wear makeup. I habitually sport tank tops because sleeves make me feel confined. I am left-handed. My favorite beverage is water—from the tap, no lemon, no bubbles. My serious demeanor causes many people to misjudge me as unapproachable and bitchy, but it is just a defense mechanism to camouflage my insecurities. Once you get to know me, I am thoughtful, creative, reliable and witty. My father taught me being early was on time, being on time was late, and being late was unacceptable. I am loyal to a fault. However, once I am betrayed, I offer little forgiveness and I certainly never forget. My love is like a matchstick. When ignited I will burn long and hot, but once the flame dies, I'm out. There is no ability to relight the fire. I take the phrase "You are dead to me" too literally. Shame and guilt have been lifelong friends of mine.

I enjoy the outdoors and keeping fit. I adore the ocean so much I joke I was a mermaid in a past life. I crave excitement and adventure. I love philosophical debates (creation versus evolution) and arguing ridiculous hypothetical situations (losing an arm in a shark attack versus losing a leg in a crocodile fight). Above all, I believe in karma.

I loathe social media—no Facebook, Instagram or Snapchat. It makes me uncomfortable. I think people focus too much on documenting and posting what they are doing instead of enjoying it. I don't care what you ate for breakfast or how cute your dog is. Thriving on likes and followers is a foreign concept to me. Being friended by people you have never met in real life doesn't make sense. I favor the exact opposite. I don't want my life on display for the world to critique and judge. I prefer to live in the present and speak to people face to face. Or maybe I just have too much to hide.

Growing up, I didn't feel particularly exceptional. I felt bland. I didn't play sports or an instrument. I didn't belong to any school clubs. I listened to alternative rock and hung out on street corners. My girlfriends were slutty, and by 14 or 15, they were sleeping around and blowing boys. I was afraid to be the butt of jokes and a subject of gossip in the neighborhood like they were, so I refrained from any sexual interaction. Deep down I think I secretly envied them for having fun. They called me the Virgin Mary and I was the prude in the group. I was a late bloomer. In eighth grade, the boys teased me because my chest was still flat. I had my first kiss at 16 with a boy on a park bench due to escalating peer pressure. I skipped my senior prom because it was a big "lose your virginity" night.

I was a chameleon and could adapt to a variety of situations. I was considered popular and had a ton of friends, yet internally, I never really thought I fit in. I constantly felt like something was missing. I hid the fact that large groups overwhelmed me and being the center of attention was my worst nightmare. I was friends with the smart kids but thought they were too nerdy and straitlaced to keep me entertained. I was friends with the troublemakers who drank, smoked, stayed out all night, and cut classes. A lot of them came from broken homes, had absolutely no guidance in their lives and had no ambition to venture out of the neighborhood. I hoped my life had more potential.

I attended Catholic school from kindergarten through high school and was raised to respect my body and myself. I was taught sex was sacred and it was reserved for someone you were in love with. My mother and father were both extremely honest, hard-working, good-natured people who made it a point to always do the right thing. Image was important. Private matters remained private. I had a slightly more skeptical outlook on life. I always expected the worst in people. I was not gullible. I expected people to have ulterior motives. I protected my feelings and only gave limited access to certain people. Bits and pieces for different people. Information needed to be earned and no one deserved cart blanche status. Those who freely paraded their personal drama with no discretion made me suspicious.

Childhood was pleasant. My family was middle class, took yearly vacations to places like Disneyland and the Grand Canyon. I never got punished or hit. Ours was a "nice" family but I would never qualify it as utopian. I don't remember ever seeing my parents hold hands, kiss or say "I love you" to each other. They were civil, but theirs was not an affectionate marriage. I suspect my parents did not have sex until they got married. We never openly discussed sex and it seemed to be an unquestionably embarrassing and inappropriate topic. As an only child, I missed out on any information an older sister would have passed down to me. I didn't understand how couples were supposed to behave in a romantic way because I wasn't around it. To this day, my father immediately changes the channel at the slightest scene of a sexual nature if we are watching TV together. He makes it so awkward.

My parents didn't understand me, but what child doesn't feel that way? One day, my mother was watching me fold my laundry and scoffed as I grabbed a handful of socks and dumped them into my dresser drawer. "Why are you so lazy? Can't you be bothered to spend five minutes matching your socks? Don't you care about anything?" Jesus, they are just socks I, thought. "I could but why should I? What difference does it make in the grand scheme of things? I could use those five minutes to do something far more rewarding." That incident demonstrated the fact that our brains operated on dissimilar wavelengths.

My parents divorced when I was 17 and it destroyed my world. I was aware they were not happy and knew it was bound to happen, but I was completely devastated anyway. Being with one instead of the other burdened me with guilt. Even though I remained close with both, I felt abandoned. The entire structure of my life crumbled.

I had been a straight A student with zero effort throughout middle and high school, but I was bored to death. I had a short attention span and never understood how history or geography would pertain to my future. I went to college because my parents forced me to. It was not up for discussion. I lived in a dorm and relished the freedom of no adult supervision. Freshman year I drank a lot and cut class occasionally. Sophomore year I partied hard and barely went to class. My grades plummeted. I was drinking and smoking weed 24/7. Weekends were spent taking ecstasy and eating 'shrooms. By junior year, I realized I needed to get my act together, so one day I dropped out and renounced my bad habits. My father was furious, and I sense has still has not forgiven me. We didn't have the type of bond that would allow me to explain I left because I was afraid I would overdose one day. To me, dropping out saved my life. To him, dropping out ruined it.

I went to culinary school for lack of anything better to do. Studying a physical trade suited me better than reading textbooks. Working made me feel productive and useful. Most important, I was downright good at it. It became my new drug. Kitchen life was fast-paced and high pressure. The competition was cutthroat; someone more talented or driven was always a few steps away from replacing you. Cooks sabotaged you, males sexually harassed you, girls competed against you. I worked hard and partied harder. My desire to be a valuable employee consumed me. I never slept. I worked long days, holidays, nights and weekends. I felt too guilty to ask for a day off and too afraid to say I couldn't stay late or pick up an extra shift when asked. I was ashamed if I made a mistake, even a minor one. I drank socially, but without the drugs, I felt a void. Then I found my next diversion—sex.

Chapter 3

Butterfly

With Elliot, I began as a naive girl, a chrysalis, but under his influence, I hatched into a hungry caterpillar. I was constantly eating, absorbing this shocking new environment and rapidly growing to expand my sexual awareness. But Elliot became the tight skin encompassing me, restricting me, so I needed to shed him.

Like Houdini, I was a shrewd escape artist. After my breakup with Elliot, I vanished. I sold my apartment and accepted a sous chef position at a prestigious hotel on Long Island to start fresh. I didn't say goodbye to any friends. I liked that no one knew my checkered history. I ignored my past. I never spoke of my past with drugs or a married man. After Elliot and I parted, I never looked back. The world of sex and debauchery disappeared. I figured it was something I did to make this one specific boyfriend happy. He had a naturally perverse side and I just went along for the ride. Mentioning these activities to another guy was out of the question. I was too embarrassed to admit the things I had done. Who would respect me?

I went back to my ordinary life and dated with indifference. Sex was never good enough. I never fully expressed myself sexually. I feared the double standard where promiscuous girls were branded sluts. I explored online dating because so many of my friends had success with it. I perused the profiles of potentials in my area with little hope. They were so generic. All the profiles sounded the same. I grew so frustrated I settled for the first seemingly nice guy who showed a remote level of interest and had a horrific six-month rebound from Elliot.

I met Roger on Match.com. He was good looking, average height and weight, and he had close-cut brown hair, light eyes, a very symmetrical face and scruffy facial hair. Occasionally his Southern accent was noticeable. Mid–30s, an identical twin, a technician for a cable company, divorced with no kids. I had been so drained from the previous depressing dates that I didn't even do my hair or shower before I met him. I had totally given up, but a friend insisted I not cancel my date, so reluctantly I went.

We met at a trendy Spanish nightclub. It was not the type of place I would normally go, but it was a convenient location. The décor was supremely white and sterile. White walls, floors, tables, and chairs. As it was a Sunday night, we were pretty much the only people there. Over a drink at the bar, we had an instant connection. Conversation was easy, and he made a lot of eye contact. I regretted not putting more effort into my appearance. I remember being so flattered that he was interested in every word I said. He agreed with all my opinions. It was like talking to a male version of myself.

Hours quickly passed and I needed to be up early for work so Roger paid the tab and walked me to my car. We kissed. Then again. And again. We couldn't stop and ended up making out in the car for another hour like horny teenagers. We spent the next few nights together. We had sex on the third date and I made sure I told him I usually waited longer to have sex. I needed him to understand I was not indecent.

The sex did not impress me, but I liked that he liked me. It was quick and boring and basic, according to my standards. I hoped it would improve. We started dating exclusively after the first week. Roger had all the qualities Elliot lacked—he wanted to spend every second with me, take me anywhere I wanted to go, meet my friends and family. He wanted to introduce me as his girlfriend. He wanted to show me his office and introduce me to his boss. It was nirvana. I felt honored to be wanted so desperately.

Within a month, we had both said "I love you." I slept at his place almost every night. I basked in his attention. He had grand visions of us getting engaged and living a cookie-cutter life. It was every girl's dream—or at least what I thought I was supposed to dream of. Maybe I would finally be able to tell people I had a man and a future. I would no longer have to explain why I was still single at my age. All these things allowed me to overlook his sexual shortcomings. Roger, unfortunately, had a major problem with erectile dysfunction. He finally agreed to take Viagra, but it only helped so much. His penis still wasn't dependable and taking a pill and then waiting for it to kick in killed the spontaneity. The fact that he needed medication to be able to fuck me broke my heart and crushed my self-esteem. I knew it was a valid condition but that did not make having to take Viagra sting any less. It stripped me of my femininity. I didn't feel like a woman. The memories of my escapades with Elliot faded and I resumed my habit of having sex as a duty. Roger always tried to pursue it, but it had no appeal. Eventually I resigned from a life of poor sex to no sex. It was less of a hassle to just avoid it. I never mentioned my secret life, and by the second month of dating, I noticed this wonderful catch had skeletons of his own.

After some suspicious behavior, Roger finally admitted he was technically not divorced. He had been separated for many years but never filed the paperwork to complete the process. No words could describe the betrayal I felt. Flashbacks to Elliot flooded my mind. Roger apologized profusely for lying and promised to get divorced immediately and he did. He does love me after all, I thought. We continued dating and then hit the next roadblock. I slowly realized Roger had a dominating streak. Initially I assumed we were together 24/7 because it was a new and exciting relationship, but I eventually realized I was wrong. I could not go anywhere or do anything without him. Seeing my family and friends without him caused vicious battles. Having hobbies that did not include him or watching a movie without him enraged him. It angered him if I wanted to walk home from the train instead of getting a ride from him. I had no personal space or privacy. I was suffocating. Escaping his company was like trying to separate myself from my shadow. All my hobbies became his hobbies. He had no friends of his own, so my friends became his. He was no longer the male version of myself. Now he was a carbon copy of me. I lost my identity.

To the outside world, we appeared to be the quintessential couple, but I frequently had anxiety attacks and cried in the bathroom. After another month or so of struggling, I hit my breaking point and confessed to my mother that I was terrified of Roger. She told me he would never change, and I needed to run as fast as I could. She demanded I leave him immediately. It was one of the few instances in my life that I remember her ordering me to do something. Instead of facing him, I went to his apartment while he was at work to retrieve my belongings and then I called him and said it was over.

Chapter 3. Butterfly

The breakup was grueling because he was not willing to let me go without a fight. I thought nothing could be worse than leaving Elliot, but I was wrong. Roger called and texted constantly. He showed up at places I hung out and tried to associate with people I knew. I saw him everywhere I went. I grew increasingly paranoid and uneasy. He relentlessly begged me to give him another chance. He swore he was a changed man and he would treat me properly. Give me the space I required. I didn't believe him and pleaded with him to leave me alone. It drained me emotionally and mentally and I became jaded. A lot of people thought I was being overly dramatic. But anyone who has been the victim of emotional/psychological abuse knows the victimizer is a first-rate illusionist. In public, he appears to be devoted and charming, but behind closed doors, he is a deceitful manipulator. I was humiliated that Roger tricked me.

After my traumatic break up with Roger, I formed my protective cocoon and guarded myself from the harsh conditions of the dating world. I completely stopped dating and refused to let anyone penetrate my personal space. I became cautious about who I let into my life because I feared I could never get them out again. I vowed I would never be a victim again. My career became an excuse to not socialize. I claimed to be too busy working to date.

I volunteered to go in early and stayed late just to have an escape. I was so focused that even after I left the building I constantly answered emails and phone calls from coworkers. Being accessible and solving problems 24/7 gave me a diversion. I appeared romantically dormant but internally I was secretly embarking on a remarkable transformation. A true metamorphosis.

As time passed, I became lonely. Around 3 a.m. on a random Tuesday in May 2015, I couldn't sleep. Nothing on TV kept my attention and I couldn't call any of my friends at that hour. I grabbed my laptop and re-joined Match.com. A few minutes later, I closed the webpage and typed in the address for the old swinger site Elliot and I belonged to. I laughed to myself, thinking, "Yeah, right," and thought better of it. I flipped through the channels on TV as my eyes kept glancing at my laptop as if it were beckoning me. Five minutes later, I typed the address in again and hit "Enter."

I'm sure most of you are wondering how one can be a swinger if one is not part of a couple. A swinger is defined as someone who has an open relationship, enjoys multiple partners and/or participates in group sex. I assured myself I was just going to look around—I wasn't *really* going to do anything. I created a free account, screen name and password. I had an unhealthy obsession with the color red—red car, red bed sheets, red dishes, red everything—so that was a no brainer, but "Red" sounded bland and dull. I tried to think of other reddish words. Crimson. Maroon. Cinnamon. So lame. Then it hit me—Scarlet. It sounded exotic and alluring. Jackpot. I added my birth year and became Scarlet1982.

I was logged on for less than five minutes with no pictures or profile description yet and I already had emails from people wanting to talk! I was shocked but so curious. One of the guys who wrote to me looked cute and seemed nice enough. I still have no idea how I had the balls to do this, but after a few texts he and I planned to meet the next day. The anticipation was nearly debilitating. All day at work I worried about my date. What should I wear? What would I say? What if I froze and couldn't even kiss him? *Am I seriously doing this?*

We met at an Irish pub in my neighborhood. I figured it was smart to be in familiar surroundings in case I needed a fast escape. An 80s rock cover band performed while a trio of old men sat at the bar watching sports highlights on a muted TV. Families enjoyed dinner in the booths along the side wall. In person, he wasn't as desirable as I expected, but he was okay. Not too cute, but not hideous either. He appeared smaller in stature than his pictures suggested and much less masculine. He stared at the floor than at me, so I assumed he was nervous and therefore harmless. The conversation was strained and there were a lot of uncomfortable pauses. I saw it as a good test to see if I could really have sex with someone I just met. Like a practice round. I didn't really know him, so I wasn't worried about having to face him the next day, which was comforting. I didn't know my capabilities back then, but I was about to find out.

Two beers later, I was bored to death. I made the executive decision to get things started. I invited him back to my place, and as we walked the six blocks there, I jammed my fists into my jacket pockets so he wouldn't try to hold my hand. I was imagining how this was going to proceed because we were both bashful. How did this work? I wished I had a procedure manual. I knew I would have to take the lead if anything was going to happen. I gave him the tour of my apartment and led him to the bedroom and turned the light to the lowest setting, just enough to see a blurry version of him. We sat on the bed and it was eerily quiet as I mustered up the courage to kiss him. I guess that gave him the signal he needed because his demeanor immediately changed. He lunged toward me and kissed me furiously, way too much tongue. Wet and sloppy. Kissing him was terrible! Like making out with a slobbering dog, I imagined. When he fingered me, it did not turn me on. It was uncoordinated and frantic as if he were digging for loose change in couch cushions. His hands were cold and tiny which creeped me out. He seemed clueless about the lack of pleasure I was getting. He was like a horny little boy who had never seen a naked girl before. He unbuckled his pants and asked me to rub his dick. It was small, and I was not too enthused. We had sex for a few minutes before he came. It was over before it began. He was new to this scene also and had no self-control.

After he left I was frustrated and unsatisfied, but I was glad that I had gone through with the evening. It was the first step. As I showered him off me, I reflected. Now I was certain I could fuck a stranger and that was empowering. I emerged a vibrant butterfly finally ready to spread my wings and master the art of flight. I went back online the next day and joined the site for three months because paying members had more privileges. I uploaded a few faceless pictures and answered the profile questions. I was on a mission now to figure things out. I quickly met several more people and soon discovered there was a lot to learn! Each experience, whether good or not, taught me valuable lessons. Most important, I learned that I could be a sexually unabashed person on my own. I did not need to rely on a man. I did not need to explain or apologize for my behavior. I could make my own path. And, if you ask me, I would say my 30s became the pinnacle years of my life. I didn't truly know myself in my 20s. I was too busy living for other people. It was a tricky road to navigate, but after three years, I became an educated swinger. This is how a cautious single girl discovered herself.

Chapter 4

Sex-planations

What Is Sex?

Sex is natural part of life. Yes, it is vital for procreation and to express your undying love for your high school boyfriend, but for me it is so much more than that. Sex is the ultimate escape. The past and future disappear; time stands still. As bodies synchronize, I am hypnotized in the present, in that specific moment, and everything else drifts away. Desire and passion are extremely powerful emotions. I no longer care that I hate my job, need to pay an overwhelming credit card bill or got into a fight with my parents. It is a mini-vacation for my soul.

Sex is a universal language. The most basic, natural, instinctive way to connect. A touch or a kiss can be more powerful than a thousand words. Your body's subconscious reaction expresses whether you like it or not—even if your mind cannot comprehend it. So why do humans overcomplicate it? When did "love" become so intertwined with sex? It blew my mind that the two did not have to be mutually exclusive. Sex is pleasure so why put so many restrictions on it? Why hinder your fun? Why make it more dramatic than it needs to be? Please don't misinterpret me as unable to love or distinguish lovemaking from fucking. I agree there are many types of sex—but my point is I did not learn the variations until extremely late in life.

I think a lot of people assume swinging is simple. Sex is sex, right? *Wrong!* Swinging can be profoundly complicated. Even though consenting adults are involved, there are personality clashes, jealousies, physical incompatibilities, equipment malfunctions and a lot of unreliability. I have had more forgettable sex than you can imagine!

You like donuts. That may sound like a clear statement, but it leaves me with more questions than answers. Do you like vanilla or chocolate? Glazed or with powdered sugar? Cream filling or jelly? Discovering what "sex" meant to other people was enthralling. Everyone's interpretation of the word is different. Does the word make you think of lovemaking? Missionary sex? S&M? Does it last 30 minutes or several hours? What makes sex good to one person may make it terrible for another.

Every sexual encounter is unique. Bodies are like snowflakes—no two are alike. Every person has a kiss as distinct as his or her fingerprint. Every penis is different. The width, the length, the curvature, the texture, the smell, the taste. That's where the thrill comes in. Nothing compares to the first time I touch someone new. It's an unparalleled high. Because each person I am with is different, I am different with each of them. I am constantly a varying version of myself.

How does an individual define a specific word? The term "rough sex," which is thrown around endlessly, can involve many different things. Would you interpret it as hard pounding? Hair pulling? Slapping? Choking? All the above? Is "kinky" wearing a nurse's costume or letting a guy cum on your face? What is obvious to you may be unclear to someone else. Do your likes and dislikes shift depending on who you are with? Can you have an orgasm from someone whose looks do not attract you?

For example, I met a gentleman who was devilishly attractive and we developed a strong chemistry talking on the phone before our date. Over a few drinks, we flirted and when I kissed him sparks flew. We progressed to a hotel room and couldn't wait to indulge in each other. Unfortunately, once we were naked I realized our tastes were dissimilar. My expectation was to fuck while his was to make love. I curiously asked, "How can you make love to someone you never met? That doesn't seem possible to me." He replied, "I like you, I don't want to just fuck you." That confused me. "But I want to get fucked," I laughed. "That's what we are here for." We compromised and had a mix of gentle sex with wilder moments. We never saw each other again.

Learning each body is like solving a new puzzle. Memorizing each person's predilections is crucial. What makes him tick? Does wearing lingerie for him get a reaction or does it go unnoticed? Does he get aroused or bothered when I talk dirty? Does he respond to a gentle touch on his cock or a firmer grip? Knowing your subject creates better sex.

Chemistry is an unexplainable phenomenon. I have found there is no direct correlation between how well you know someone and how compatible the two of you are sexually. I have had some of the best sex of my life during first encounters while several guys I built stronger connections with have left me surprisingly disappointed. The quality of sex did not always guarantee a repeat encounter for me. I could have stupendous sex with someone, but lacking a connection beyond that, it was one-dimensional. I called that "hollow" sex. It was pleasurable but not sustainable. Or the sex might be mediocre, but the personal connection was so magnetic that it balanced out and I saw the person again. The latter option was more enticing than the first.

For me, becoming a swinger was like anything else in life—practice makes perfect. I treated swinging like cooking. To create a delicious dish (satiating sexual experience), I needed the proper ingredients (the right people), a sharpened knife (keen intuition), and a willingness to experiment with assorted seasonings (various scenarios). Then I could develop a proper recipe (my fantasy).

Swing Time

The word "swinger" has a certain connotation and portrays outdated stereotypes. Many people associate swinging with an earlier decade, key swapping parties, porn mustaches and shag carpeting. In fact, it can be hard to point us out. Believe it or not, I look just like a regular person. Most of my friends would be baffled if they knew I was a swinger. I would guess that most of them are not even aware swinging is so prevalent now. Swingers refer to sex as "playing."

Sex was a huge part of what drew me to this world, but the people were even more fascinating to me. I liked to get inside their heads. Why did they do it? How did they get started? What were their boundaries? What were they searching for? How did they describe their involvement? Swinging taught me to be more tolerant and accepting of others as well as of myself. My type had always been "clean cut, athletic white guy" but I grew to appreciate the beauty of different body types and skin tones. Think about it—if you are having open-heart surgery, do you want the sexiest doctor or the most capable one?

Although swinging does involve couples swapping partners, it is not limited to that. I call this the swinger pyramid. Imagine a drawing of a triangle. Single Girls (highest, smallest tip) are the most desirable but extremely rare, referred to as "Unicorns"; Couples (middle layer) have a strong presence; Single Guys (largest bottom tier) are available in abundance. Two singles can hook up, a single can join a couple for a threesome or multiple people can engage in an orgy.

There are many variations of swinging which allow an individual to choose the level that suits him or her. Another appeal of the Lifestyle for me is that I am forever changing; I can proceed as slowly or quickly as I wish. I sample and decide as I go. I change my mind. I grow with the Lifestyle. It takes a flexible personality to go with the flow and adapt to situations. I always expect the unexpected.

Swinging can be a minor part of life, just a little excitement. Some people occasionally participate in the sex aspect in between regular relationships but don't necessarily consider themselves swingers. Those who enjoy the physical part but also observe the values and code of conduct identify as "in the Lifestyle." New people are "Newbies" and those who have been around are "Experienced, "Seasoned," or "Veterans." Some people stick to NSA (no strings attached), and others prefer ongoing encounters and become FWB (friends with benefits).

Some people refuse to play with others who live in their area because they are afraid they will know the same people. They want to keep their identities more private and don't want their covers blown. I prefer local "playmates" because logistically it is easier to meet more frequently or on short notice. I am all about convenience.

I was in Shoprite buying groceries and noticed a familiar-looking guy looking at lettuce in the produce department. Did I know him? I think I fucked him during a threesome. As I browsed, I tried to casually get his attention by coughing. Nothing. I continued shopping and texted him. "Are you in Shoprite?" "Yes," he replied. "Me too. Meet me in the pasta aisle." We reunited with a warm hug. He said, "You changed your hair." I said, "Yes, I am impressed you noticed." Later that day I went to his house and fucked him.

Most of my partners lived about an hour or an hour and a half away and were worth it. Quality outranked distance. Others used the site when they traveled for work or went on vacation. I got a lot of emails saying, "I will be in your area for these dates, can we please meet?"

Swingers are some of the coolest people. Situations that would be outrageous to regular people are just normal to us. Just as a doctor becomes desensitized to the sight of blood, I did with nudity and sex. If a coworker asked you what you did over weekend, you might respond, "I went to Trader Joe's, had dinner with my friend and caught a movie." Perfectly normal answer. A swinger might say, "I went to my kid's recital, did laundry and watched my wife fuck five black guys." To me—still a perfectly normal answer. Trust me, if you ever meet a swinger, have a conversation with him or her. Swingers have the most outlandish stories! But don't get me wrong—there are a lot of assholes in the Lifestyle, just like anywhere else.

Whenever sex is involved, there will be drama, immaturity and stupidity. Rejection brings out the worst in some people. They showered me with compliments to get noticed, then, after a tactful "No, thank you," I instantly became a tramp. I have honestly told people "Go to hell" or "I wouldn't fuck you if you were the last person on earth," yet the next day they asked me to hang out as if everything was copacetic. I've had to block numerous people from my profile and cell phone because they harass me. These people clearly don't belong in the Lifestyle.

After work, I met a guy for drinks. We had been texting for a few days although I was not sure I would like him. His pictures weren't drawing me in and the conversation on the phone wasn't very interesting. His voice sounded serious and boring. We lived very close, so I agreed to meet just to get out of my house. I wore yoga pants, a button-down shirt and mascara. I looked nice but was not trying to appear overly sexy or eager to fuck.

The minute we hugged hello I knew for a fact I was not fucking him, but making a new friend and having a drink was perfectly fine. He did most of the talking in the beginning and I tried to act interested in what he was saying. I studied him. He looked like an average white guy, mid-40s, slightly thinning hair. He did not give off any sexual energy or a flirtatious vibe. It was difficult to even imagine him having sex, let alone being involved in the crazy world of swinging.

I sipped a glass of wine and he ordered an appetizer. He was cutting the quesadilla and somehow the knife slipped out of his hand and crashed to the floor as food and sour cream sprayed his shirt and the area around his plate. This guy was so uncool. A little awkward. I was starting to get tired. This was not good company.

Suddenly he turned to me and asked, "So how are things going so far?" I laughed. I thought it was a joke. He said, "No, seriously. How am I doing? Are we getting a room?" I paused, and he glumly said, "That's not good." I tried to be affable, saying, "You are very different than the guys I normally meet." "How so?" he asked. I racked my brain to choose non-offensive words. "You are more laid back and reserved, I guess. I am used to more energetic, flirty guys." "So you would like it better if I had my hands all over you at the bar? I was trying to be respectful." "No, it is more about the energy you give off." He said, "Trust me. I have a wild side." "Noted," I replied.

I went to the restroom, and when I returned, he asked for the check. "What now?" he asked. I shrugged my shoulders. "We could get a room," he offered again. My silence answered that. "Or I could walk you to your car," he added. I conceded. We walked down the street and I felt the tension of rejection thick in the air. As we approached my car he stopped and declared, "I'm just gonna do it" and grabbed my face and kissed me. I do not know why but my reaction was laughter, which made kissing hard. I think it was because I did not expect him to be aggressive. The kiss was not that bad, but I still felt zero chemistry.

I pointed to my car, said good night and things got weird. It was as if he had a moment of panic, knowing me getting in my car was very final. He grabbed my hand and kissed me again. Let's get a room. No, thank you. Come back to my house. Absolutely not. Desperation was setting in. I could see it clearly in his eyes. He begged me to let him eat me out in my car. No fucking way. I was beginning to get irritated now. I said, "Wow, you are a completely different person from the quiet guy in the bar." "I told you I had a wild side. There's just a time and a place for it," he replied as he pressed me against my car and kissed me as he squeezed my tits. I pushed him away. "On my car in front of CVS is most certainly not the right place either." He grabbed a handful of my hair and tried to rub my pussy. "Just over the jeans," he said, as if that was acceptable. He assured me I would love how he fucked me. He was one of those guys who was confused about what being dominant meant. I had no doubt I would not like fucking him. My tone was growing angrier as my patience was severely tested.

This other side of him was bizarre and not well received. I looked him in the eye and said, "Don't be that guy." "What guy?" "That creepy guy. It's not cool." He apologized. Trying to diffuse the situation, I offered, "Call me sometime." He said, "Why do I have the feeling I will never see you again?" "Keep acting like this and you won't," I confirmed. He put his hands on me again and I said firmly, "Enough. I am leaving." What the fuck is wrong with these guys? What girl finds this attractive?

Eventually I was safe in my car, alone. As I drove off, I chuckled. This may sound twisted, but every time I told him no, or removed his hand from my body I got stronger. It was like a can of spinach for Popeye. I got home, and he texted me to say he had a fantastic time. He immediately followed up with a picture of his dick. What an idiot. I did not respond.

Survival required a thick skin. I had to submerge my romantic, sensitive, sentimental nature. I learned to cope and not let myself be broken down, but I won't lie—once in a while, I was crushed. I definitely had nights that left me bleak or crying and feeling like shit. No wonder single girls were often labeled crazy or bitchy. This shit was overwhelming! This world could tear you down and destroy you if you let it. Insecurity was like a shark smelling blood in the water—dangerous.

I met Roberto at the bar at 8 p.m. He was ten minutes late because he had to stop at the bank. I was slightly nervous because he was not my normal type. I couldn't tell from his pictures if he was light-skinned black or Spanish. Something in his eyes drew me in but I wasn't sure if I would be attracted to him in person. This was a gamble.

Roberto walked in and I was immediately at ease. He was even more attractive in person. He was six feet tall, had tan skin, was very muscular, and he had a close-shaved goatee and a very warm smile. His large muscles were obvious through his form-fitting shirt. We ordered drinks and the conversation started very vanilla then casually moved toward Lifestyle. We had similar experiences and both wanted to date someone in the Lifestyle. His personality was laid back but funny and genuine. His eye contact was serious. Something about him reminded me of my old playmate Vincenzo. Maybe his smile, those big plush lips. Maybe the way he laughed.

I noticed him check his watch and I said sarcastically, "Oh, do you have somewhere else to be?" Roberto said, "No, I can't believe we have been here for over an hour. It feels like I just got here. I guess I really enjoy your company." I blushed. We continued talking and had a second round of drinks. He suddenly confessed, "I need to try something," and he leaned in to kiss me. What a superb kisser. Soft lips, very sensual. When our lips parted, he asked if I wanted to get out of there. "Yes, just let me go to the restroom."

I splashed cold water on my face. Damn, he was sexy. I returned and he paid the tab. We walked down the block to a nearby park and sat on a bench. The weather was too nice to be inside. We chatted for a while before he kissed me again. This kiss was more intense. I melted as he ran his fingers through my hair. We proceeded to make out on the public bench as people walked by. "I never make the first move," he whispered. "Oh I need to ask you to fuck me?" I asked. He laughed and said, "I don't like to pressure anyone but, just so you know, I am dying to have you." It was 11 and we both needed to be up early. We had to make a decision. Not an easy choice but we agreed it would be rushing tonight so Roberto asked if we could continue tomorrow night. I said, "Absolutely."

As soon as I got home, Roberto called to tell me once more he had a wonderful time and was excited to see me again. He was pleasantly surprised by our chemistry and was thankful he met me. I was honestly a little giddy. Not fucking that night just added to the anticipation for the next night.

Motherfucker. He stood me up. After all the bullshit about how he wanted a serious relationship and was looking forward to exploring one with me he bailed on our date at the last second. Ugh. I hated guys sometimes. Why on Earth would you put so much effort into pretending to like someone? Why not just be honest? Or, better yet, why not get laid and then not call me back? It just didn't make any sense. I texted him to say thanks for being like every other guy and playing games. Nothing made my blood boil more than deceitful people.

Even with the craziness, the benefits and the excitement from swinging heavily outweighed the nonsense and frustrations. Finding that diamond in the rough was *sooo* worth it. It was just so damn exhilarating. I spent the majority of my time with males in the Lifestyle, so it was a refreshing break to grab dinner or get a pedicure with a vanilla girlfriend for a dose of estrogen to help maintain my equilibrium.

Common Questions

What is my sexual orientation? I am straight. How can I be straight if I play with women? I am not attracted to women and I never crave being with them sexually. I would never date a woman and I would never play with a woman alone. I would never invite a single woman to join me and my guy, but I would play with couples that were a package deal. I am bi-friendly meaning my primary focus is the male but if the woman is bisexual I am not repulsed interacting with her. Kissing was usually a given and I was fine receiving oral from a girl, but I never performed it in return. That's where I drew the line. I could look past her gender and enjoy the pleasure she gave me. Besides, once my eyes were closed, a mouth felt like a mouth—no matter if it was attached to an X or Y chromosome. If I turned her on, it added to the overall fun of the situation, especially because the male was definitely turned on. It's like a non-smoker having a cigar to celebrate a friend's new baby. One or two cigars a year doesn't make the person a smoker. A woman here or there didn't make me bi. At least that's how I saw it. I would never pass up a dick for a vagina. Ever. If the other woman was straight, we alternated fucking him and blowing him. Either way it was a fun variation from the norm.

Does swinging make me polyamorous? A vanilla friend asked me this and my initial response was absolutely not. After some research, my answer is I am not exactly sure. The word "polyamorous" encompasses a wide array of non-monogamous practices. For me, there is a vast area where swinging and polyamory can overlap but they do not always coincide. When I was with Elliot, I was in love with him and no one else. He was the key male in my life and I never had reoccurring relations with any of the other men.

This question is not as cut and dried as it may seem for a single girl. One-night stands do not represent polyamory for me, but the fact that I have numerous open sexual relationships with emotions involved may qualify. I never identified myself as "poly" because I am not in love with my partners and we have no formal labels on our relationships. If I were to have a real boyfriend again, I anticipate him being more important than anyone else I fucked. He would take priority and would be the only person I was in love with. So I would categorize myself as a swinger with slight poly tendencies while I am single.

Am I a sex addict? No. I can solidly reject that notion for several reasons. An addiction is something that consumes you and you have no restraint. It causes you to be helpless, reckless and unable to make logical decisions. Consequences are ignored and safety is jeopardized. While swinging is all about being carefree sexually for me, I want to clarify that it is different from being careless. I am extremely selective with whom I play. Swinging and being highly active does not mean I fuck anything with a pulse. I turn down a lot of sex and I invest a lot of time seeking out the right partners. I am deliberate with my actions and seriously weigh risk versus reward. My actions may appear spontaneous, but I analyze most things I do. Reading profiles and sifting through possibilities can be a full-time job for me. I take sharing my body with another person quite seriously.

*A Sample (*Balanced*) Week in My Life*

Monday: work, gym, Lifestyle date (drinks with a new person, sex at hotel if I like him)
Tuesday: work, gym, laundry, catch up on my DVR, pay bills
Wednesday: my day off—morning Lifestyle date (sex) at hotel with a regular, gym, wax/pedicure, dinner with a parent
Thursday: work, dancing with my vanilla friends
Friday: work, wild Lifestyle date with a regular (sex—maybe a club or a threesome, then breakfast)
Saturday: yoga, work, dinner or movie with vanilla girlfriends
Sunday: gym, work

It's feast or famine sometimes. Three Lifestyle dates a week is ideal to keep my hormones balanced. More than that could get out of hand and take over my life. After being very active for an extended period, I needed to take a break. It got overwhelming at a certain point and sex took a lot of energy out of me. I briefly stepped back and evaluated my real life. Were there any friends I hadn't seen recently that I should? Was I sleeping enough? Had I abandoned the gym or my other obligations because sex was more important? Was my laundry basket overflowing? Sex less than twice a week was boring, especially if it was all one-on-one sex. Then I felt too vanilla! If I went more than a week without sex, I felt like a born-again virgin.

Safe Sex

Before I started swinging, I was in monogamous relationships and didn't use condoms. Swinging was the opposite—we were all sleeping with *a lot* of people, so condoms were essential. I always wanted to be prepared and not rely on the man. I remember being so embarrassed buying my first box of condoms in CVS as an adult because it was so new to me. I thought the sales associate was judging me. I bought a bunch of other items to mask the discomfort. Later, I had no shame marching to the counter with my date and only buying a box of condoms, clearly announcing we were about to go fuck.

I was insanely fretful about catching an STD. I never had one and wanted to keep it that way. I made sure my partners wore condoms and I got tested regularly at the clinic. I religiously swallowed my birth control pill at the same time each day. While most girls hate their monthly visitor, I welcomed mine. It meant my investment in the pharmaceutical industry was money well spent. There were a ton of shady guys who "forgot" condoms or claimed condoms killed their erections and tried to coax you into playing bare. To me that was a sign that they did not care about their own health, let alone mine.

Once I was naked in my bed with a guy. We were getting along famously and kissing heavily. As he was about to go down on me, he paused with his face a few centimeters from my vagina and asked if I had an STD. I shouted, "Absolutely not!" He made some comment about how he wouldn't be upset if I did because due to my high sexual activity it was logical to assume I did. I was outraged. (1) He had all night to ask me about my health records. This moment was way too late for that discussion. (2) He said he wouldn't be upset. That statement made me even angrier because it sounded like he would totally fuck a girl with an STD! I was so disgusted. I got dressed and kicked him out.

As I started getting more comfortable with long-term partners, I became more lenient. The goal was to always start with condoms, but if we became steady playmates, we would eventually elect to lose them.

It was a sign of faith and privilege. In a few isolated cases, the first encounter I had with a guy was so hot and steamy we never even had a chance to think about using them even though I had them in my bag. That was not ideal, but shit happens. In other cases, I always used condoms even if the guy was a long-term partner. There was no concrete system anymore. I always tried to pick partners who seemed "clean and selective" like myself. I avoided profiles that advertised bare back sex as a preference. Only two guys have been granted the distinction of being allowed to cum inside me. That was the ultimate display of faith.

One day a close friend, whom I never used condoms with, called me because he was suffering from burning during urination and he was convinced he had chlamydia and had gotten it from me! I was outraged! I had no symptoms. "I am clean," I kept saying. "I am selective." I apologized a million times, hung up and cried. I immediately scheduled an appointment at the clinic and got tested plus I got a shot for chlamydia just as a precaution. I was freaking out. Who gave it to me? How long had I had it? Who else had I infected? I was mortified at the thought of calling people to break the news I gave them an STD. I was devastated. For a week, I was a wreck waiting for the results. When they finally came in, they were negative. Mine and his—no chlamydia. I was so relieved.

I vowed to myself never again would I have unprotected sex! That was my big wake-up call. This may sound bizarre, but demanding to use condoms made me feel more proper, less slutty. Like it directly related to how I was viewed according to social and moral standards. A few weeks later the memories of panic faded, and I resumed having unprotected sex with *select* partners. Let's face it, raw feels better and is more intense. It is a judgment call taken very seriously. To this day, I have avoided contracting an STD and I plan on keeping it that way!

Chapter 5

Split Personality

In the vanilla world, I tried to present myself as the girl next door. I suppressed my sexual nature so I could be respected and viewed as a "good girl." A guy earned the right to have sex with me and I might stall until I felt ready. I did not lead with my sexual-ness to avoid being labeled "trashy." Sex made me vulnerable.

I was a small fish in a giant pond. One in a million of similar girls. My culinary qualifications and accomplishments did not get me respect from the male cooks under my supervision. Having a vagina was a disability. In my parallel world, laws of gender reversed. Being a unicorn gave me the superiority I craved. I became a big fish in a tiny pond. My vagina was a priceless treasure that men were on a quest to discover.

In the Lifestyle, I created my alter ego Scarlet. Scarlet was a work in progress. Swinging contradicted everything I was taught so it was an arduous process to retrain my brain to separate sex from the person and the physical from the emotional. Through trial and error, many failed attempts and numerous poor dates over the years, Scarlet developed into my interpretation of a sexual Wonder Woman. Scarlet was your dream girl. Feminine, dominant and aggressive. She had no patience for those who did not value her. She was admired and respected for it. Her sexual prowess was a sign of power and not weakness.

At first, Scarlet was still enormously my vanilla self and easily affected. This world was so new and exciting to me! I was unprepared for the amount of attention I received. I never considered myself beautiful, but a lot of these people did. I was not graceful when I received compliments. I had a perfect athletic, hourglass figure, yet I blushed when guys called me "hot" or broke eye contact when they com-

Chapter 5. Split Personality

pared me to a model. I wished I could see myself through their eyes and little by little I did. When a potential prospect didn't show up or the chemistry was lacking I took it personally. If the sex was not good or the guy couldn't get hard or came too fast, I presumed it was a direct result of something I did wrong. They must not like me. I must not be good enough or sexy enough. When dates did go well I expected there to be a text the next day. Proper conduct eluded me.

I realized if I was going to continue in this world and not lose my sanity, I needed to get acclimated fast. My encounters became research and data collecting so I could study and master the art of swinging. There were so many potential people to meet; I didn't have enough hours in the day. I strategically planned my life around swinging. Three weeks out of the month I was active. Week four, when I had my period, I packed my schedule with activities with friends and family. Sometimes I would fuck multiple people in one day as if I were scheduling business meetings. My life revolved around it.

I kept track of who I fucked on a calendar in case I got pregnant or caught an STD. I probably fucked more than 100 people from when I joined in May until the end of the year. I was like a kid in a candy store and I wanted to sample every flavor. I was mostly into straightforward one-night stands. I would meet the guy or couple for a drink, fuck, and leave. Having great sex made me hornier and the next day I wanted more great sex. Bad sex just made me want to fuck someone else to replace it with great sex. Either way, I never had enough sex.

I probably fucked a lot of people who would not make the cut now. I wasn't knowledgeable enough then to distinguish between the true swingers and the horny posers. My bullshit radar was not on target. A handful of the people I fucked in the beginning were more interested in their pleasure. Guys who wanted me to suck their dick but didn't go down on me. Guys who were only good for a quick fuck. Couples who seemed to really be secure but turned out to have trust issues. The first few couples I met had arguments in the room once we got naked. One girl swore she wanted to watch her husband with another woman but became suddenly jealous. Was it because I was younger and in better shape than she was? I was usually five to ten years younger and had never given birth. I worked out constantly and was in fantastic shape, with a large chest and plump ass. Playing with me was a little different than playing with a housewife. I was also a threat because I was single and available. Did I want to steal her husband?

Year one was tremendously educational. I learned what I liked and didn't like. I figured out how to pick more appropriate matches. I made it clear that meeting me in person was not a binding agreement to fuck me. I reserved the right to reject you at the bar or in the room. And most important, I gained the ability to assertively tell people what I wanted. Instead of being there solely for their pleasure, I learned how to make it more about what I wanted. My modesty soon faded, and I seized authority over my sexual destiny. Scarlet blossomed, my attitude changed, and the tables turned as I stopped taking responsibility for other people. I started to feel beautiful.

Year two I found some level of balance. I was still highly active, but I did not let swinging interfere with my regular life. I would meet people after the gym instead of skipping the gym, after I had dinner with friends instead of cancelling on my friends. I tried to limit myself to a certain number of playmates a week. I still had a lot of one-night stands but started having more ongoing encounters. Until then, I wasn't aware that was an option. We regarded each other as people, not just bodies. My regulars ranged from once a week, every other week, once a month, and so on. Some of them were even on actual schedules, as in every Wednesday at 11 a.m. we met at the same designated hotel. Others were available specific days so, for instance, they would be my Monday or Tuesday guys. Most were random; when we had time or were in the mood we would coordinate.

My intuition improved, and I became extremely selective, concentrating on quality over quantity. Finding people who were more interested in the overall shared experience or, even more surprisingly, people whose main goal was to give me pleasure. True Lifestyle guys honestly get the most joy out of giving the woman satisfaction. They seriously wanted to make me the center of attention and give me the best experience they could. This was such a new concept to me. I was no longer afraid to admit what I wanted or correct something I didn't like. I became much more vocal.

Now I assumed if a guy didn't get hard he must be too intimidated by me. If he came too fast, it must be because I was too hot for him to handle. If he didn't fulfill my needs I felt bad for him. He was just no

Chapter 5. Split Personality

match for me. He was an amateur. If sex were a sport, Scarlet would be a heavyweight champion. While I was uncomfortable being naked in the gym locker room Scarlet reveled in nudity. The only characteristic Scarlet and I shared was a goofy sense of humor. No matter how I tried I could not disguise my passion for corny puns and *Seinfeld* references.

Scarlet was a wolf even if she sometimes disguised herself as a sheep. With a little practice, she became someone who was self-reliant and in charge. She knew what she wanted, was not afraid to speak her mind and commanded attention. She was highly sought after and left an impression. Instead of requiring a drink to lower her inhibitions, she preferred to fuck completely sober so that she could savor every moment and relish each sensation. She didn't want to dull her senses; she wanted to heighten them. She wore racy, revealing outfits, felt at ease parading around in skimpy lingerie, and, according to several people, had "fuck me eyes."

I had extremely high standards and have been fortunate enough to fuck a lot of talented superstars. It has been a blessing and a curse. I had sex on a level that most people dreamed about, or maybe even better than they could imagine. But since I was spoiled, essentially, the bar was set so high for the new guys that it was almost impossible to meet. It is like tasting Dom Pérignon—once you experience it, all the other champagnes don't quench your thirst. They may be decent, but you always compare them to the Dom and they never quite measure up. Sex was like that for me.

Scarlet became so fierce that if she was not being pleased to her liking she would stop midway through sex and leave. She had no regrets. *She was her own priority.*

I received an email from a guy who was in my area for the day on business and wanted to hook up. I had seen his profile before and he was drop-dead gorgeous. He was Italian, five feet, nine inches tall, had gelled-back, jet-black hair, crystal blue eyes and the body of an underwear model. Yes, I wanted to meet! After a few short e-mails, we agreed to meet at the pizzeria down the block from me. It was early afternoon on a weekday and he only had a few free hours, so a hotel rendezvous wasn't practical.

His face was strikingly beautiful, almost like a porcelain doll's. He ate two plain slices and drank a Coke while I watched. I wasn't hungry, but we needed to get acquainted briefly before I allowed him in my house. Basic protocol. He was not overly talkative and low energy, but he was fucking hot and I had nothing else to do.

As we laid naked in my bed my sensors started to go off. He was touching me, but I wasn't turned on. I found it unusual that he was not heavy into kissing. The interaction felt too routine. There was no passion. In my mind, I debated my options. Finally, I tapped him on the shoulder and said, "I'm sorry but I feel like something is wrong. I am really attracted to you, but I am surprisingly not turned on." His reaction gave me the indication that girls usually didn't object to him. He apologized and offered to be more sensual. We started fooling around again and he finally kissed me. It was awful. Uninspired.

I interjected again. When I reiterated my concern over the lack of chemistry, he rolled his eyes. I sat up and asked him a critical question. Are you attracted to me specifically or are you just looking for a warm body to fuck? He stared at me with compete confusion. As if I was speaking a foreign language he could not understand.

A long pause followed, and with my arms folded, I said, "Answer the question." He shrugged and confessed he didn't care who I was. He just wanted to get laid and the girl was irrelevant. That sent me over the edge. I jumped to my feet and said he needed to leave. He was baffled and asked me to reconsider. I shouted and pointed to the door as I tossed his clothes at him. Like a scolded dog he avoided eye contact as he hastily dressed. That day I learned the most priceless lesson. It is never too late to say no or change my mind. I was proud that I stood up for myself. I had a voice.

Whenever I tell this story to other swingers, they are fascinated. They give me so much credit and consider me a bad ass. Most people would muscle through the sex and just never see the person again. Not me. There were no more mercy fucks in my world.

Year three I basked in the glory of being an almighty unicorn. I was seasoned. The more sex I had the bolder I got. I had solid friendships with several singles I saw regularly and intermittently met new ones. I was a master at seeing through people's bullshit and an expert at determining who I wanted to meet. By now, I had fucked so many people I could barely remember them all. Often, I would come across a profile online and it would jog my memory. I would think, "Oh yeah,

Chapter 5. Split Personality

I fucked that guy." Must not have been good if I had forgotten. I hated being insufficiently pleased and viewed it as a heinous offense. I would rather wait longer periods in between sex for people I really wanted. It was better to have one phenomenal date than three mediocre ones. Perhaps I was a sexual snob. My fantasies escalated to fucking multiple guys and picking up strangers at clubs. Sex was my nourishment. It fueled me. It was just as important as oxygen.

Chapter 6

Me versus We

Single females are referred to as "Unicorns" because they are viewed as mythical creatures due to their limited number. Unicorn status was a double-edged sword. I was particularly marketable, sought after by both single males and couples. As usual, when a product is in high demand, it becomes more valuable. For many, being chosen by me was rewarding; they appreciated the rare opportunity to spend an evening with me. It was like a winning lottery ticket for them, which was gratifying for me. On the other hand, I often felt like there was a target on my back. Some people wanted to fuck me just for the sake of conquering a Unicorn. Bragging rights. Like mounting a deer head on their wall. I was a collector's item. I am sure some girls would be pleased but I was offended. I loved partaking in people's fantasies, but I refused to be a trophy. It was demeaning.

Early on I learned just how powerful Unicorns were. Thankfully, someone told me because I had no clue! Unicorns could pretty much have whatever we wished. We made the rules, we chose who, what, when, where and how. We could be bisexual or straight. I enjoyed perks like having access to any club or party (usually for free) and I never paid for drinks or hotel rooms. After a lot of trial and error, I enforced my requirements for a first meet; potential partners must be willing to travel to my area and get a hotel. I had candidates drive three hours for a chance to fuck me. That was quite an ego boost! Once I was comfortable with them—and they had proven to be stellar sexual partners—I had no problem traveling to them or going to their houses or hosting them at mine.

Some girls with single profiles were not in fact single. They were married but played alone, which I personally feel prevented them from being true Unicorns. I never had much direct contact with other single girls, so this is all hearsay, but I heard a lot of them on the site were crazy, not that attractive, unstable, got too attached or couldn't handle the pressure. (I'm sure there are exceptions—there must be other girls like me.) I was too insecure in the beginning to socialize with them. I needed to adjust myself to this new life and I needed to do it on my own. I didn't want to be influenced or judged by or compared to them. I wasn't extremely bisexual, so I had no urge to play with them. Plus, the negative ways most people described them didn't make becoming friends sound too appealing. I was concerned they would be jealous or competitive or try to sabotage my connections. I received emails from girls who played with the same guys as I did, warning me to stay away. The main comment I always got from people was how normal I was, down to earth, just a regular girl. Why couldn't more single girls be like me? It was quite flattering.

Being single and staying sane was nearly impossible. Constantly giving myself to people with no formal relationship could get tiresome. I wanted to protect the bonds I created. It was difficult not to become territorial with the fellas I had strong connections to and stressful knowing I was sharing them with other girls. It was crucial to remember variety was the point of this and their interactions with other girls were not a reflection of their feelings toward me. I was doing the exact same thing to them, after all.

A good friend used to tell me four was the magic number. Most connections were one-night stands. You may meet partners again, but if you could get past the fourth date, then just maybe it would last a little while. Aside from chemistry, I think timing was key. Say you buy a candle that can burn for six hours. You can light it once, let it burn for six hours and enjoy it once. Upon lighting, the scent is strong, but by the sixth hour, it may not even be noticeable because your nose has adjusted. Or you can light the candle in one-hour increments on six different occasions. Each time the wick ignites, you get a new burst of the fragrance.

Seeing the same person frequently over a short period could make the excitement wear off fast or cause you to get attached. Waiting too long after the first date could get you or them lost in the shuffle of other new people. Hooking up with a partner every two to three weeks seemed to be the sweet spot for me. It was just enough time for me to miss him but sex still seemed fresh.

Even the closest ties could vanish with no warning and I had to accept each moment could be the last together. Some people disappeared and resurfaced with explanations. Others permanently vanished with no warning. There was never 100 percent security even with those I trusted most. Friends with benefits could seem like friends but turned out to be more like "acquaintances." Real friends stick by your side through thick and thin. Fake ones only hang around until the benefits run out. But vanilla friends can be guilty of that as well. If you think a regular relationship takes work, try balancing several fake ones at once. Swinging relationships are a million times harder.

I grew to view interactions like a bouquet of fresh-cut flowers. They always begin as a beautiful gift that brings a smile to your face and makes you feel special. They smell wonderful and the colors are bold as they bloom to their potential. But no matter how attentive you are, the clock is ticking. The minute the flowers are cut, they start to die, whether you realize it or not. Rot and decay are inevitable. I know it sounds cynical, but it is realistic. Just enjoy it while it lasts. The friends that stick around longer are like potted plants, rooted in soil. You work hard to maintain them. You nurture them, trim their dead leaves, give them fresh water and sunlight. Just know sometimes you will be the one thoughtlessly disposing of the dead flowers, and, unfortunately, other times you will be the dead flowers thrown out like garbage. That's life.

Adjusting from a couple to a single girl had its positives and negatives. I was a five-foot, four-inch girl going on dates with strangers from the Internet, so safety clearly became the main issue. Meeting was high adrenaline and higher risk and I missed having Elliot by my side to protect me. With him, I was 100 percent carefree. He was my bodyguard. Generally, males were more respectful with him around because they didn't want to piss him off. As a single girl, I found they could forget their manners and were too pushy or demanding. Of all the times Elliot and I partied at sex clubs, there was only one experience that scared the shit out of me.

We wanted a change of scenery so instead of going to our regular hangout we ventured to a new one. The club was located on one floor

Chapter 6. Me versus We

of a random office building in the downtown area. Most of the clubs had the same basic things, just varying layouts. It was a smaller-sized place with a coat check immediately through the entrance. The main area consisted of two leather couches positioned under a large flat screen TV playing porn. There was a small folding table to the left with food and snacks. Beyond the seating area was a freestanding bar where patrons dropped off their alcohol. The bartender labeled the bottles with the patrons' names to keep them organized. The club provided cups and mixers.

Straight ahead were more couches on the left and a stripper pole in the center of the room. Bathrooms were to the right. Continuing the tour, we found a small area with tiny lockers and finally the play rooms. There were three rooms of similar sizes with mattresses on bed frames. Two rooms had two beds and the other had three. We had arrived early so no action was taking place yet.

This event transpired early in our swinging days before we understood that different clubs had different types of clientele. Elliot and I chilled on the front couch and people-watched. As it got later, the club got more crowded. We were not impressed with the general appearance of the people who had shown up. They were older and less attractive than we wanted. Eventually some couples started playing in the back rooms. Stationed by the front door we had the first view of everyone who entered.

An older man and a younger woman walked past us. He was in his late 40s, was bald, wore glasses, looked Eastern European. She appeared much younger, late 20s or early 30s, and she reminded me of an old movie star with her shiny black bob, pale, flawless skin, bright red lipstick, and tight black dress. They walked over and sat on the couch across from us. I can't remember their names, but I will never forget what happened.

Introductions over, they asked us to play. We were technically a soft swap couple, but I was not attracted to the man. We agreed to play but Elliot made it clear that the involvement was restricted to girl-girl play. "No problem," they said. The four of us found an empty bed in one of the rooms with two beds. I was naked and she was topless. She and I started kissing and touching and Elliot occasionally touched my hair while the other guy watched. Both of the girl's hands were on my face when I felt another hand caress my thigh. My body jolted. I looked, and the guy was groping me. I casually moved my leg away from him and refocused on the girl. I felt the hand again, pawing at me. I was getting annoyed. I whispered something to Elliot and he politely reminded the man I was not interested. A few minutes later, I felt a firmer grab on my inner thigh. Before I could complain, Elliot grabbed the guy's hand and warned him not to test his patience. I was getting a little edgy, but the other girl was unfazed.

She was kissing me again when I felt a hand violently inserted in my pussy and I didn't know what I expected to happen, but I sensed it was not going to be good. It happened so fast I have difficulty remembering every detail. If I close my eyes, I can visualize bits and pieces. It still gives me chills. Elliot's loud voice. That temper of his. His hand around the man's throat. The man's glasses hanging crooked on his face. Blood trickling from his nose. The girl's shrill scream. My own voice begging Elliot to let go. Tears running down my face.

How did our fun evening just turn into a crime scene? Within seconds, the commotion got the entire club's attention. Couples surrounded the mattress. Women watched in horror, appalled, while the men attempted to pry Elliot's hands from the man's throat. I prayed Elliot wouldn't kill him. When he was angry, it was impossible to snap him out of it. He was locked on the guy like a lion on a gazelle. It took three men plus one bouncer to separate them.

As his hands released I let out a cry of relief and threw my arms around him. The bouncers escorted the man away as the woman scrambled for her shirt and scurried after them. Elliot was trying to calm himself down and some women wrapped a sheet around me as they comforted me.

Jack, who intervened, was also a regular at the other club. He recognized us and that's why he helped. Jack also told us the couple we met were not a couple—she was an escort. Apparently, some single men hired prostitutes to act as their dates so they could gain entrance to couples-only clubs. It wasn't extremely common, but it did happen. Elliot asked how he could tell. Jack said it was a combination of appearance and attitude—their large age gap, his cheap clothes versus her expensive-looking clothes and the lack of affection between them. It made sense now. That was why he was so disrespectful and didn't obey the "No means no" rule. That night I learned people are not always what they seem and you can't take people at face value. You need to read body language and pay attention to the small details.

Elliot shook Jack's hand. I got dressed and washed my face in the restroom. The bouncers and the club owner swarmed us. Were we okay? Were we sure? Did we need a doctor? Did we want to press charges? A flurry of questions. They guaranteed that couple would be blacklisted from any future events. They swore nothing like that had ever happened before. They were sincerely apologetic. Naturally, we did not want to press charges. That would make a wicked headline—"Married Man and Mistress Almost Kill a Man at a Sex Club." No, thank you. My parents would have died of embarrassment.

After that, we took a break for a few months. Elliot was okay, but I was traumatized. We eventually started going out again because we missed it, but we were much more careful and aware of who we engaged.

This frightening incident never left my brain and I thought if it could happen with Elliot, what could happen without him? What if I got raped? My first few dates, I was so paranoid meeting strangers that I left a note hidden under my pillow with the screen name and location of my date. I figured if I got kidnapped or killed my room would be searched for clues. I vowed to be careful on my own but in hindsight I put myself in situations I regretted because I simply didn't know better. With every experience, I got smarter and more composed.

After experimenting with every scenario, I realized I should not go to another person's house on a first meet. Feeling trapped made me feel too vulnerable. As well as I vetted these people they were still strangers. I watched a lot of true crime TV and horror movies so I always considered the fact that this person could have a dungeon in the basement or a hidden video camera or a friend planning to join us without my permission. I hosted at my apartment many times because comfortable surroundings made me feel secure. I knew the exit strategy and I knew where the knives were. That may sound extreme, but I had to be realistic. However, kicking someone out was also strenuous. I had three scary situations as a single girl that I will share throughout this book.

First scary night. I invited a guy to my house for our second date after our first night at a hotel was a success. We had just finished fucking and planned a third date. As we laid in bed, we got into a conversation about other guys I was seeing. His demeanor shifted as he ranted about all the other guys, whom he had never met, being pathetic losers. He bragged they would be no competition against him picking up girls at a bar. This guy had issues. I told him he was out of line and his temper rose, so I started to get nervous. His volume increased, and I attempted to calm him but couldn't. I told him I had to be up early for work and I needed to get to bed. He accused me of trying to kick him out and I swore it was just getting too late. He finally got dressed and I walked him to the door. He kissed me goodbye and said, "See you Saturday," to which I responded, "Have a safe drive." I was so relieved to have him out of my house but concerned because he knew my address. Thankfully, I never heard from him again.

Hotels became my preferred first date spot because they were public, and in case of an emergency, I could cause a scene and get help. Neither party had the advantage at a hotel plus it added to the excitement because it felt more sordid. People used hotels for affairs and hookers, so they seemed like the right places to have wild secret sex. A hotel also added a level of protection to your identity. No one knew who you were or where you lived so a person's ability to crash your vanilla world or interfere in your daily life was reduced. Another bonus to hotels was I didn't have to constantly wash my sheets and I could be rowdier and louder without disturbing my neighbors, but I digress.

Another negative aspect of being single was it could be lonely and hard to stay grounded. Elliot was my gravity. He was the constant. The center of my world with swinging rotating around us. Without him I lost my balance and got swept away, being pulled in directions by every person I encountered. A shitty night single could be depressing. If the sex was bad, then I went home alone and unsatisfied. As a couple, it became a ludicrous story that you bonded over and you could always recover the night by fucking each other. There was a camaraderie over shared experience. It brought you closer because you shared this secret. Even with consenting adults, the outcome of the night was like playing roulette. Personalities clashed, body parts malfunctioned, people got wasted, there was jealousy—my experiences ranged from completely mind blowing, to hilarious, to mediocre, to shocking, to utterly disappointing. Sometimes, I missed having a teammate. I had to train myself to find stability on my own. My anxiety was also much worse without him. Entering a room full of strangers was less threatening when I was with Elliot. I was able to block it out because he was my barrier. Most swingers were surprised when I admitted my disability because I was so friendly one-on-one. But even after three years, I still suffer from attacks when I attempt to attend a party. It always starts out with a positive attitude and good intentions but eventually I end up with shortness of breath, jittery hands and sweaty armpits. It's definitely the one major battle I still can't overcome, so I am honest about it.

Hiding the fact that I was a swinger was much easier when I was dating Elliot. Having an official relationship to offer the general public gave me an easy answer when someone asked what I did last night. I hung out with my boyfriend. End of story. Being single changed it from a fun secret to a laborious secret. Now when someone asked what I did last night I had to create elaborate stories. I am not a homebody so claiming I stayed home on a Friday night was unlikely. Saying I went to a movie led to more questions—Who did you go with? What did you see? First, I hate lying. Second, it was hard to keep my lies straight.

The biggest benefit to being single was I did what I wanted. Simple. I didn't have to ask permission or make apologies. I didn't take one for the team (sleeping with a guy I didn't like so my partner could fuck his female in exchange). I didn't have to worry about upsetting my partner or disagreeing on who we wanted to play with. I didn't have to follow any previously agreed-upon rules. I could change my mind in a split second without conferring with someone. For once in my life it was all about *me* and *my* desires. I was the highly coveted Unicorn.

Sharing ... How Can You Do That?!

Swinging boils down to one thing—sharing. Whether you are a couple sharing your partner or you are a single and sharing yourself, it is a unique thing to do and perhaps not for everyone. A couple must have a strong foundation and reassurance because sharing magnifies your relationship's weaknesses. Swinging to fix a marriage is like having a baby to save one. It is plugging a leaky pipe with a wad of chewing gum; it won't last.

For me, I only found swinging erotic because we were committed. Once our sex reached a certain peak we needed more. It was like graduating from alcohol to weed to pills to heroin. You always needed the next bigger high. It was almost like bragging. My man is so hot/sexy/skilled, I'll let you borrow him but then he is coming home with me. It was easier to share something that was mine because I knew I would get it back.

One night my friend Joe and I went to a couple's house and they were nice people but not exactly hot. Joe and I were on the couch and they were across from us on a loveseat. Drinks were poured, and friendly conversation ensued. I went to the bathroom and when I returned the wife was sitting next to Joe, which forced me to sit beside the husband. Ah, sneak attack! I was not into him but wanted to be amiable, so I didn't complain about the new arrangements. We played a card game, and as I shuffled the deck, I saw Joe and the wife kiss. I was going to kill him! In response, the husband touched my leg. I cringed and continued messing with the cards to avoid the situation. Now the wife and Joe were ravaging each other, and I knew that meant trouble. He just opened the door for me to be fair game and didn't notice me giving him the death stare. The husband kissed me as he tried to put his hand down my pants, but I swatted it away. Joe's pants came down and she sat on his cock. He jumped up, flipped her over and pounded her. The husband was growing more daring as he attempted to fondle me again and I lost my patience. I pushed him off me and yelled, "Joe, bathroom—*now*," like you would scold a child. He fumbled to pull his pants up. Once we were alone, I told him I wanted to leave. "What's wrong?" "I am not fucking that dude. Let's go." The car ride was tense and mostly silent. I finally said, "What is wrong with you? What happened to being a team?" He apologized and admitted he got carried away. We argued and didn't speak for a few weeks.

That night I understood having good chemistry one-on-one with a guy did not automatically make us good candidates to partner up and a lot of guys wanted to use me for their benefit. They wanted me to be their date to get into clubs or to swap with other couples who wouldn't play with single guys. I became ultra-sensitive to this. From that point on, when I partnered with singles I had strict rules. I was to be treated like his wife, meaning I made all the decisions and there was absolutely no guarantee we would actually play with anyone else. We needed to be on the same page and neither did anything without the consent of the other. And most important, they could not get angry if I indirectly cock-

Chapter 6. Me versus We

blocked them (they couldn't fuck another girl because I wouldn't fuck the other guy). I was honest and told guys up front that I was probably not their ideal partner in crime.

Swapping was fun, but it didn't turn me on in the same way because there was no ownership. I could never hear from him again. I'd rather just have him to myself than share him. Besides, I never found the other guys to be better than mine. It could feel like downgrading and was not worth it. I usually got the short end of the stick in the deal.

Once a couple wanted to meet me, but I was only interested in the husband. The wife was not willing to let me see him alone, so we compromised by inviting a single male I knew to occupy her. We agreed on separate beds in the same room. My friend immediately started banging the wife and she was screaming very loudly. The husband could not focus due to their commotion and wasn't able to maintain an erection. It almost became a competition. Which couple was having more fun? Not us. Which girl screamed louder? I never even moaned. Which man was superior? Clearly not him. His ego was bruised so he kept begging me to not give up because he was so desperate to please me. My body had shut down by then. I had to tell him to let it go eventually because forcing it was so unsexy.

While the fantasy of group sex and the ability to fuck people other than your spouse sounds fun and sexy, the reality of it can be quite different. It takes a certain type of person to have zero jealousy. You could theoretically swear your loyalty and certainty all you wanted, but testing it was real. It may be your wildest dream to see your partner fuck someone else, but are you honestly prepared to witness it? Will it bother you if some random dude makes your girl cum harder than you do? What if he has a bigger dick? If some guy calls your wife a whore as he pounds his cock into her will that turn you on or will you judge her? What if your man fucks a girl prettier or skinnier than you? What if she will do things to him you won't, like swallow his cum or anal? What if she fucks him longer than you do? What if he makes her scream louder? Are you seriously going to be okay with that? Remember, you can never un-see or forget watching your partner do filthy things with another person. If you don't in fact enjoy it, can you move past it? Can you honestly live with that?

Too many couples try to limit their partners and restrict their pleasure. They want them to have fun but not too much. They want to see them please but not more than they themselves can please. A true swinger is not affected by any of these circumstances. In fact, he or she is genuinely turned on by them. They truly want their partner to receive the maximum pleasure from the experience.

Playing as a single also has an element of sharing, which may not seem as obvious. How comfortable are you giving your body to a complete stranger? Can you really get naked within five minutes of meeting him? How affectionate are you willing to be? Is it exciting to be the third person when playing with a couple or is it scary and overwhelming? Are you just their toy for amusement or do they appreciate the role you play in their fantasies? Are they using you for selfish reasons or are they concerned about your satisfaction as well? Are you okay having sex with someone who has no responsibility to call you the next day or even acknowledge you are alive? Most experiences were isolated (one-night stands). Originally, that was the hardest part for me, understanding sex could be so final. Once we put our clothes back on that could be the end of our association forever. Eventually I began to prefer that.

Chapter 7

A Different Flavor

Vanilla (regular) dating and Lifestyle (non-vanilla) dating are polar-opposite worlds—from attire to behavior to conversation. These are typical examples of first date conversations:

Vanilla: Where did you grow up? What are your hobbies? What do you do for a living? Do you have siblings? Lifestyle: Do you like anal? Can I cum in your mouth? Are you waxed? Can you squirt?

It was perplexing for me to find my place in the world knowing both sides. I was eternally torn. I craved the stability and affection of a vanilla boyfriend but the excitement and kinkiness of a Lifestyle guy. Often, I had both screens open on my computer simultaneously, being two separate people in two separate worlds on two separate sites. PG on one and X-rated on the other. My own Dr. Jekyll and Mr. Hyde. It was tiring and tortuous. I worried I would never be truly happy in either world. It was like being trapped in a revolving door.

Vanilla guys didn't excite me. I went on a lot of first dates, hardly ever any seconds. It was necessary to remind myself that there was more to life than sex and that going to dinner or a movie with someone who was not expecting to fuck me after was sometimes sweet. It made me feel normal for a moment. It was just a façade. I felt like they would die if they knew the real me, and what I have done.

Vanilla dating was beyond boring! It was repetitive, mundane chitchat. Pretending to be more successful and settled than you are. Vaunting your accomplishments and goals. The purpose of a vanilla date is to begin something. You hope it has long-term potential. Looking your best, trying not to say the wrong thing. There is also an unwritten or unspoken rule you shouldn't have sex on a first date if you want the relationship to develop. It is not proper. If you do, then you are easy and won't be taken seriously. Therefore, these dates end with a hug or a kiss and a lot of sexual frustration.

In vanilla dating, several dates may be required for two people to determine if they have a connection. You reveal a lot about yourself and your life to see what you have in common. It requires a lot of time and information. In the first three minutes, I am wondering if I could have sex with this person exclusively. What would happen if I told him the truth? How sexually open is he? I am a passion driven person and I have dating ADD so I rapidly lose interest if there is no immediate second date.

When I did sleep with a vanilla guy, I was a little more apprehensive. You typically build up to it and sex is a big deal in taking a relationship to the next level. It represents something. You worry whether you will be compatible and like the same kind of sex. How would he view me the next day? Would he even call? It could make or break your relationship. Would I be his girlfriend now?

It was hard to have regular ordinary sex without the craziness of the Lifestyle. I could be committed but I still wanted to retain some of the fantasy world, have out-of-the-box sex and explore together. Honestly, sometimes after a lame vanilla date, I went online to meet a guy for sex. If a vanilla guy didn't want to see me again or didn't call me after a date I was devastated, it was so personally offensive. He did not appreciate the *real* me. It hurt. If a Lifestyle didn't call me back (and trust me, it was super rare—I usually had to fight them off with a stick), it didn't bother me as much because I was offering a small glimpse of a crafted personality. Scarlet was a character I played. It was just sex, purely superficial.

Lifestyle dates were the complete opposite of vanilla dates and so much more invigorating. I equate a first Lifestyle date to the fourth vanilla date. You skip the bullshit and get to the juicy stuff. We knew why we were there. There were no false pretenses. Even with no promise of sex, knowing it was a plausible possibility was hard to beat. The evening was the goal. You did not think beyond the next few hours. The "future" was not on your radar. You thought of instant gratification. The adrenaline. The curiosity. The pleasure. No two dates were the same. My night could go in a thousand unpredictable directions and that was the beauty of it, a night to remember whether good or bad. I might meet

Chapter 7. A Different Flavor

a guy at a bar, a hotel, my apartment. I might fuck him within five minutes or we might have so much fun talking and flirting we hang out for five hours and then fuck. Maybe he won't get hard, we have sex for ten minutes or four hours. Maybe one round or six. The variety and mystery were the draw. Lifestyle dates were also more convenient because I could meet people for sex at random hours or for specific times. I could arrange dates around my hectic schedule. I chose how much time I dedicated to a person.

Initial physical attraction was critical. Sometimes I met a guy based on one email and other times we exchanged several or even texted. It depended on the vibe. If I had a really good feeling about someone and we had a strong connection, I would discuss our sexual preferences and what we planned on doing beforehand. When we finally met, we were ready to explode with tension. Sometimes expectations were met, sometimes they weren't. If it was someone I wasn't sure about, I met them with little conversation because I didn't want to get my hopes up. It would all depend on chemistry in person.

I could tell in the first three minutes of meeting someone whether I would sleep with him or not. It was always awkward telling someone I didn't want to, I had changed my mind, or I just wasn't feeling it. It was disappointing, for sure, but the longer I had been doing this the easier it got for me. I was not a toy. I was not here for the guy's amusement. I was in charge of my body and I always had the final say.

It was unbelievable how easy having sex with strangers became. You met to have sex and developed a bond after. Strangers were completely open and free sexually. Sex was a lot of fun because there was usually no judgment and partners were willing to explore and try new things. Whatever your inclination or fetish, there were countless people with the same interests. Strangers had no filter and no reluctance. Being naked was comfortable. Having sex was a contained experience. I was much wilder because I knew I never had to see this person again (unless I chose to). There was not even an expectation of a phone call or text the next day, which took the pressure off.

I laughed to myself when I realized, in the vanilla world, I avoided sleeping with guys my friends dated or slept with out of consideration for their feelings. It was an unspoken hands-off understanding. Could you imagine calling your best friend and saying, "I had such a rough day. Do you mind if I fuck your husband to unwind?" In the Lifestyle sleeping with the same person as your friend was common, expected, even arranged. It was like getting a referral to a doctor.

How men spoke cracked me up. A lot of heterosexual vanilla guys won't even admit other guys are attractive, let alone comment on their bodies or rate their genitalia. Straight male swingers, however, talk about it all the time with no hesitation. They would tell me, "So-and-so has a monster cock. You would love him" or "That guy has a tiny dick—don't even bother."

You may wonder why I didn't date a vanilla guy and introduce him to the Lifestyle. For me, this was a terrible idea. I did not feel comfortable introducing someone to this world, knowing the toll it has taken on me. I thought saying, "Hey, I love you, but I'd love to fuck other people—in front of your face" put too much pressure on a new relationship. How would I convey that message to someone who doesn't live this life? I doubt it would be well received. Would he be secure knowing I have slept with most of my male friends? Would he expect me to cut off contact and make a choice? Plus, I have been doing this so long, slowly prepping a guy to get to my level would be an extra challenge. You can't just dive headfirst into an orgy. Elliot and I started even; neither of us knew anything and we learned together. Also, the fact that most swingers admitted leaving the Lifestyle after being exposed to it was nearly impossible made me feel responsible for opening a door that could not be closed.

So why not date a Lifestyle guy? Truthfully, that scenario was equally tricky. Whenever swingers met me, they were in disbelief that this beautiful, charming Unicorn was single. How had no one captured me yet? I seemed like a dream come true for a guy. Some guys were cheating on their spouses and some were in open relationships with permission to play separate. The ones who were single wanted to have fun with me but not enter a committed relationship; I think some feared they couldn't satisfy me long term or knew what I did and assumed I could not be loyal. Others refused to date a swinger, preferring a purer girl to take home to Mom, which was unfair because I was still a good person. Some wanted to date me just to upgrade their status from "single" to "couple." The majority just truly enjoyed NSA and wanted to remain single. Why buy the cow when you could have the herd for free?

Many were coping with a past break up, had commitment issues or simply led busy lives with crazy work schedules and didn't have the time for a real relationship.

Even if I met an available single guy we wouldn't automatically make an ideal couple. Yes, sexual compatibility is obviously very important, but a healthy relationship needs to be based on more than that. The sex could be spectacular, but we might have nothing else in common. Maybe we had no shared hobbies, opposing political or religious beliefs, different taste in music and movies, or conflicting views on where we saw ourselves in five years. Maybe we had some of these things in common, but the sex was just not good enough to last.

I never dated a single Lifestyle guy so I'm not sure how our viewpoints and preferences would intertwine. I hadn't shared a guy I loved in more than ten years. What if I did suddenly get jealous? We could be compatible one on one, but were we into the same type of swinging? Did he want to remain in the Lifestyle or leave it if we dated? Were we willing to compromise or were we stuck in our ways? What if I hated every girl he wanted to fuck? I liked fucking multiple guys—what if that turned him off once I was his girlfriend? Could I still speak to my other male partners/friends if we were dating or would I have to let them go to keep him? Would we play with old partners or have a rule that we start fresh and only fuck new people together? Would we have the same standards and tastes when choosing other couples?

My Profiles

My Match.com profile portrayed me as innocent and virtuous. I had the obligatory smiling face pic to exhibit my cheerful personality, full body pic to show I'm not fat, a group shot to prove I have friends. I checked off the boxes for my preferred interests—hiking, exercise, dining out, movies. How original. I tried to attract a wide range of suitors by using words like "outgoing, adventurous and family-oriented." I cast a wide net for maximum responses.

On the sex site, I was straightforward, explicit, and specific about what you must be to get my attention. I looked for particular types and tried to narrow the candidates. Standard requirements were males under

45 with fit bodies, dominant with great stamina. Couples must be equally attractive and have no restrictions. They must be willing to travel to me, no exceptions. No face pics, no credits (I will explain these shortly). Free members had no chance of being selected. Asking me for X-rated pictures or saying crude and demeaning things guaranteed a rejection.

My pictures didn't show my face; they were of my body, in lingerie or partially naked. I listed my sexual fetishes and the types of sex I liked. Preferences changed depending on my mood. Perhaps I was currently only looking for white guys, couples, or two males who were friends for threesomes or seeking a new ongoing partner, and so on.

My tone shifted the longer I was on the site. Originally, it was sweet and hopeful. Next, it became funny and sarcastic. Then it changed to serious with a hint of annoyance (examples are included at the end of the book). I had zero tolerance for bullshit. Newbies often commented idiotic things like "Man, you are demanding," "You sound terrifying" or "Why are you so negative?" They were clueless. Seasoned swingers, however, would congratulate me for my straightforward demeanor, call my perspective refreshing and sympathize with my plight.

Secret Stress

I wrestled with shame, keeping my swinger life extremely private. Was I biologically predisposed to it? Did I unconsciously choose it? Was I subliminally influenced by outside forces? I tried to leave the Lifestyle, but I always came back. Why did I need it? I only confessed my secret to three people and it was terrifying. Luckily, they were all understanding and could separate my sexual preferences from the rest of me. They did not judge although they were totally shocked. I mean, of course! I do this shit and yet I look in the mirror sometimes in disbelief.

Amy, Marcy and I had been (vanilla) friends for two years. During one of our routine gossip sessions, I mentioned I needed to tell them something and made them swear not to freak out. I had a speech memorized but the words stuck on my tongue like glue. My face turned red and my body temperature rose as they stared at me, waiting. Once I said the words "I am a swinger" out loud, I exhaled a sigh of relief. Marcy's demeanor remained neutral, but Amy's eyes were enormous,

Chapter 7. A Different Flavor

and her jaw fell open like a cartoon character's. They were incredibly fascinated and inquisitive about this elephant in the room. They asked questions and I answered candidly. Sharing stories felt like I was replicating the plot of a movie I watched or repeating a story someone told me. As the words came out of my mouth, it sounded so outrageous that I participated in these events. How could I have two such contradictory personalities?

I have grown to accept this part of myself as just another hobby I have. I like antiquing, I like running, I like swinging. I have specific friends for each of activity. Part of me had no problem and wished I could be more open about my life. Having a double life was 50 percent fun because it was taboo and secret. The other 50 percent was taxing because I was hiding. I valued honesty. Lying about my whereabouts and concealing my Lifestyle associates weighed heavily on me. I always pondered the consequences of being 100 percent truthful, all the time, with everyone.

Why does sex matter so much? Why are people so afraid? We all have it. My sex life should not define me—but does it? Why does sex spark so many unfair judgments? I noticed when there was a sex scandal in the news or a graphic sex scene in a movie people had aggressive, often hostile opinions. If you found out your child's second grade teacher was a swinger would you be disturbed? Would you suddenly find her less suitable to teach math? If you discovered your mother and father were swingers would you be disgusted? Would it take away the admiration you had for them? I fear losing a lot of respect and relationships—especially my parents. What would their reaction be? Anger? Embarrassment? Will they disown me? Will they ever forgive me? How will I ever be in a room with them and not be uncomfortable? Will my friends no longer welcome me around their husbands? People often associate promiscuity with disgrace, but what I do naked should have no impact on any other areas of my life. It is simply a personal preference. I am financially sound, have a good job, and own an apartment and a car. I have a good heart and I am caring. It doesn't make me any less intelligent, reliable, funny or successful. It changes absolutely *nothing*.

Taking it one step further, how will people react to this book? Amy and Marcy were kind enough to assist with my writing aspirations, but I don't expect their level of cheerleading to be widespread. Even if other people could accept me confessing my secrets privately, how will they feel about me broadcasting them to the world in print? I try to guess which friends will read it. If so, would they admit it or deny it? Who will ask me questions and who will ignore the book's publication? Will they support me or refuse to spend money on what they call smut? Do they have the capacity to understand why this is an important topic? Can they see past the sex and appreciate my emotional journey?

Swingers always say someone should write a book about this shit. Will they be amused that I did just that? Will fucking the famous Unicorn be their new game? Or will they avoid me for fear of being in my next book?

How will I feel once this information is public? Writing quietly in my apartment was easy, but having my words in print for anyone to see is scary. How do I even broach the matter? The jump from chef to sex author is not one people expect. Do I warn them and I send a massive email blast saying, "By the way, here is the release date for my new sex memoir." Will I gloat about being an author or downplay it because of the subject matter? Will my parents be proud or mortified by my success? Will they see me as a resilient woman, who, despite doing drugs and dropping out of college, had the tenacity and skill *to write a fucking book*? Or will they not be able to see past the fact I wrote about sex? Will the topic negate the accomplishment? What if my shining moment is mistaken for my biggest failure?

Chapter 8

Swinging Systems

The origins of swinging are debated. I Googled it and several articles speculated swinging was prevalent among military folk because officers promised to look after the wives of their deceased brothers. Other articles suggested it was a direct result of the sexual revolution of the 60s along with the invention of contraception. Either way, it seems swinging originally consisted of wife swapping with friends or at least with people who had something in common. Somehow it shifted to swapping with strangers. Older swingers reminisce about how complicated meeting others was in the past. It was hush-hush. They had to know about secret locations or know someone who knew where to go. In this digital age, however, the Internet provides easy access to everything. And yes, there is an app for that!

Now before you call me a hypocrite for using a social media site, let me explain. A sex site is not the same as a social media site. I am not living in a virtual world. It is just a means to an end. The purpose is to ultimately get offline and meet real people in real life for a specific reason, while remaining discreet. It is anonymous whereas most other forms of social media are all about advertising who you are. After I sampled several swinger sites, one became my home base. I loved lying on my couch in my PJs hunting for my next target—it was like Amazon for sex. It was convenient as I could be online while I ran errands, did chores or even sat on the toilet.

The Site

Profiles had pictures and written descriptions. Public galleries could be seen by anyone; private and personal galleries only by invitation.

Private was generally face pictures and personal usually contained more graphic images—images of dicks and pussies and even action shots of people having sex or getting blow jobs. Normally when you go on a vanilla date having sex is the first time you see a guy naked. In this world, it is the opposite. I have seen most guys' dicks before I've ever said a word to them. You could see who viewed your profile, send emails, IM chat and even review (credit) other members.

Personal settings (which could be changed constantly) explained whether you were straight, bi or bi-curious as well as indicated your level of interest in meeting males, females or couples. There was a section to describe yourself, list your experiences and your fantasies. Some profiles were explicit and others generic. I didn't interact with people who had blank profiles. To me it meant they did not take this seriously.

Unfortunately, a fair amount of profiles were fake. Guys posing as couples, people just wanting to collect pictures, or those getting turned on talking but who never intended to meet. There was also no screening process to join the site so there was a wide array of members. Not everyone looked like Ken and Barbie. The beauty scale ranged from one to ten. You had your choice of early 20s to late 70s, six packs to beer bellies, clean cut to covered in tattoos, natural bodies to fake tits, silky smooth bodies to insanely hairy.

The "Naughty Date" sections let you search for events and hookups. Members posted their locations along with the time and the type of situation they were seeking. For example, I may write, "I am a single female in [insert city here] looking to meet a couple or single male who is willing to host at a nearby hotel. Free after 7pm. Please be under 45, in good shape, no smokers and credits preferred. Must provide face pics when responding."

The site also listed parties and special events at clubs and guest lists. You could check attendees' profiles to see if you might like them, maybe contact them and plan to meet at the event.

The site offered three forms of membership. Free members had restricted access, could not see private galleries, give or receive credits and were limited to five emails a day. Paid members had all access and perks and paid a monthly fee. Lifetime members received all the benefits but paid a one-time fee, which saved a lot of money. A lot of people, including myself, judged your degree of sincerity by your level of membership. I rarely responded to free members because I assumed they were not as invested in this world as a paying individual. They claimed, "I'm just scoping it out before I invest money in it" or "I want to see if this is real before I sign up." The site was so inexpensive paying members saw that as a cop-out. A lifetime member earned the most credibility. I started with a three-month paid membership because I thought this was just a short-lived phase. After renewing my membership several times, I realized I was invested in this. I did the simple math and I was wasting a lot of money, so I became a lifetime member.

Credits

One of the most hilarious features of the site was the accreditation element—"credits" for short. It was literally like Yelp for sex but only positive ratings (although I wished negative ones were allowed sometimes!). You wrote reviews about people you met and posted them to their profile. Again, this differed vastly from "liking" a post on Facebook. If a person posted a picture of a birthday cake hundreds of people may click the "like" button. But what did that mean? They were not necessarily anywhere near that cake. They didn't touch it, smell it, taste it. So how much weight did their opinion carry? Credits, on the other hand, were much more authentic. It was customary to only use the person's first initial to keep his or her name private. The person could then accept or deny the credit. Credits could be deleted at any time by the writer or the recipient. They could be brief sentences or practically novels. Credits were a debatable topic.

Some people refused them because they wanted their escapades to remain private. I was originally on this train. It seemed sketchy having your exploits posted, but that plan could backfire because being totally anonymous made you questionable and riskier. Credits, therefore, made you credible, proving you were who you claimed (that's why I eventually allowed them) and you had physically met other people face to face. You could be accredited by another member or the host of a club or event, which would allow you to see if you shared mutual acquaintances; a credit was like an unofficial reference. For some people, on the other side of the spectrum, credits were bragging rights. This was all they cared about. They wanted to fuck you just for the glory of another notch on the bedpost. A male friend told me a girl he knew was getting fucked doggy-style by a guy and he kept screaming, "Credit this!" If I had been that girl, I would have ended the sex immediately. To me, the guy's behavior was tacky and immature and a major red flag. Proper etiquette dictated you should never ask for a credit. If you had a great time you could write one and the other person may or may not write one in return. End of story.

Credits ranged from "G was polite and good looking"—pretty basic, not a lot of information, but at least you know he showed up. "C has a good looking, great package, stamina is unbelievable, he gave me multiple orgasms"—informative but still respectful. "F's cock is so big I could barely fit it in my mouth and he came so much I almost choked"— whoa. TMI. I refused to post anything graphic or tasteless. I had numerous guys yell at me because I didn't accept their credits or because I wouldn't write credits for them. So childish.

I reckoned a credit was a recommendation that the person I met was *safe*. It reduced the risk of being cat-fished. Therefore, I only wrote credits if guys were reliable, looked like their pictures and were respectful. Although not required, I only credited people if we actually had sex because, to me, this was a sex site. I have deleted credits I wrote because I deduced the recipients were liars or cheaters.

Once, I had fucked a guy four times before he confessed he had been using a false name so his wife wouldn't find out he was cheating. Another time, I fucked a guy at a party. He was gorgeous and there was an intensity about him that I loved. His performance was not stellar because he couldn't stay hard, but we just clicked. A few days later, he reached out and said he wanted to fuck me again. I suggested we make a game plan and he responded by telling me he would love to, but the hour drive just wasn't worth it because he was an alpha male. Outraged, I gently reminded him that he was lucky I even offered a second chance due to his inability to please me fully. He did not appreciate that! I made my share of enemies, but reputation was important to me. It may seem petty, but it was the only way I could regain a sense of control of a situation where I felt wronged. It was justice.

I limited my credits because you could be judged by them in more ways than one. I know, it gets tedious. (1) Credits have dates. Some people were turned off if they saw you had multiple ones from dates very close together. On the flip side, if all your credits were from ten years ago, it aroused suspicion. I questioned why there was a gap and wondered if a person's photos were current. (2) An exceedingly high number of credits might portray you as skanky. I had sex with more than 300 people, but *documenting* I had sex with 300-plus people seemed over the top! I capped my credits at 30. When I accepted a new one, I deleted my oldest one. (3) I don't know why, but other people, especially single guys, were obsessed with mine. They stalked my profile and tracked me. I received emails from random guys demanding to know why I chose that guy over him. Critiquing my selections, questioning the dates because I said I was busy. It became absurd! (4) Other users could see who wrote the credit, click on his or her profile and judge the merits of the writer and the level of taste they had. I turned down so many prospects because I didn't approve of the people they slept with prior.

Reading credits was entertaining, though, and it was like the Six Degrees of Kevin Bacon—at some point, everyone I slept with was linked, like a twisted sexual soap opera. The website had tens of thousands of users, but within our state, we crossed paths with all the same people. Good fuel for gossip! I loved hearing others talk about meeting people I have been with. You learned whose genitals smelled funky and who was lame in bed, who was a force to be reckoned with and who could not hack it.

In my early days, I attempted to branch out to meeting couples. It was hard to find the right pair, and after a few failed attempts, I thought I had found just the one. Two of my closest male friends were credited by the couple and confirmed they were super cool, laid back people. We met for drinks. Fast forward to me in their basement. The wife insisted she wanted to see me fuck her husband, so I did. Within a few seconds, she flipped out and stormed upstairs with no explanation. The husband chased after her and I was dumbfounded. I had no clue why she freaked out, but now I was trapped in their house, alone, naked and terrified. I threw my clothes on so fast, they were still inside out. As I put my shoes on, the husband stomped down the stairs and notified me the party was over. No kidding, I thought, just get me the hell out of here. He led me to the front door and shoved me outside with a look of panic in his eyes. I bet he was in for a major fight. I sat in my car in the driveway and cried until I stopped shaking enough to drive safely. That was my second scary night.

I called my friends the next morning and yelled at them for misadvising me. Their responses were shock. "Hmm, I guess it is different for a single girl," one offered. "Maybe the wife got jealous because they normally only played with single guys." I was the sacrificial lamb to appease the husband. This was when I understood the importance of knowing a couple's history. Having credits from only single guys was a major piece of information I overlooked.

Social Swinging

Sex sites are not the only way to find swingers. Swinger-friendly establishments are everywhere. You can Google them and find their websites in seconds. There are two types of events: on-premise and off-premise. On-premise means nudity and sexual activity is allowed—and encouraged! These are your sex clubs. Certain nights have designated access and rules. Saturday nights are usually for couples and single females only while Thursdays or Fridays might also allow single males.

The energy is drastically different on special nights. Couples nights are fun and friendly, very social. Single guy nights generally consist of a ton of single dudes congregated around the beds like vultures looking for prey, dejected, hoping someone will invite them onto a bed to join the action. The desire and desperation in the air are palpable. The couples in attendance these nights are typically women who love multiple guys. The single guys are generally there because they couldn't find a date.

Clubs are discreetly located in obscure buildings with no signs. You would never know the club existed unless you were specifically looking for it. Some are small lofts with just a few beds, some are abundantly spacious, occupying multiple floors. Overall quality ranges from sketchy to high class. Most have theme nights like "Naughty school girls," "Bi night," "All white party." Holiday parties for Halloween and New Year's Eve are popular. Clubs are BYOB, and some provide lockers and towels. Certain clubs require you to undress and change into a towel or robe to enter the designated play areas while others allow you to remain dressed.

Chapter 8. Swinging Systems

Clubs have always been captivating to me because of the crowds. I'm strictly an exhibitionist. I'm there to show off and be watched and make the other people wish they were in my position. Knowing they were turned on, knowing they wanted to be a part of the action was my adrenaline. Voyeurs are the opposite. They watch. Watching did nothing for me. I'd rather be having the fun than watching it! It is surprising how many people go to clubs just to watch. They hang out fully dressed, having a drink, just watching other people fuck. I guess it was like watching live porn.

Those who do play either play with the partners they came with but enjoy the thrill of having sex in public. Others go with the purpose of fucking other people. You could have sex with as few or as many people as you want.

Typically, clubs have a mix of public play areas (mattresses in open areas/anyone can see and join) and private play rooms (closed room/must be invited in). If you are playing on an open bed other people will slowly flock over to you to get a better view; they may stand around the bed, sit on the edge, try to touch you and ask for permission to join. You say yes or no. You may have several couples on one bed playing separately or they may all play together and have an orgy. Another amusing part to me is the crowd reaction. After top-notch performances, they would commend you, shake your hand and say, "Thank you" or "Wow, I enjoyed that."

Some clubs are open to anyone while others are exclusive and require you to submit photos to get on the list and still others require memberships. Fees vary for single girls, couples and single males. Discounts may be offered to members of a site or for arrival before a specific time.

Off-premise is considered a "meet and greet." A regular bar or restaurant will be reserved for swingers to socialize and get introduced, but they do not allow playing. Usually, it is inside or near a hotel, so attendees can play after.

People also throw small hotel parties and private house parties where anything goes. There are also a lot of resorts, cruises and other vacation getaways specifically designed for swingers.

Although it can be entertaining to go out occasionally, I prefer connecting through the site. Going out required a lot more effort and did not always yield equal benefits. I had to get dressed up and travel to the location. It was a time commitment as events generally opened around 10 p.m. but didn't get crowded until 11 or midnight and continued until 3 or 4 a.m. There was no guarantee I would like anyone there, so it could be unproductive. I could dedicate seven hours of my life and not have sex. Those were not enticing odds for me. Plus, there was always the possibility my social anxiety would kick in and I would shut down.

I also preferred smaller settings because I liked intensity. Imagine you add a drop of purple dye to a cup of water. The water becomes a dark, deep purple. The water represents the number of people and the dye the atmosphere, the level of emotion. A twosome or threesome will be focused and intentional. Now take a gallon of water (a party or club) and add a drop of dye. The water will only be a pale lavender. The larger the setting, the more diluted the experience becomes for me. Attention drifts and concentration is easily disturbed. There are simply too much surrounding stimuli.

A Proper Introduction

Whether in person or online, propositioning a stranger for sex takes a certain level of expertise. There is a fine line between forward and offensive, polite and wimpy, confident and arrogant, aggressive and disrespectful. Finding the perfect balance is rare. Some people are way too blunt and come off as disrespectful and crass. Others are too timid and overly polite which takes away the sexiness. Both will lose my interest immediately.

How do you pick someone up at a club? The customary code for initial contact is same sex. A single girl should approach a couple by engaging the female half first. It is important for the women to connect before involving the man. A single man should always introduce himself to the male half of a couple simply as a sign of respect. The male half of the couple would then direct the single guy to speak to the female since she is the one who would make the decision. A main rule is the woman has the final say.

Connecting electronically means you can't see facial expressions or gauge tone of voice. Sarcasm often gets misinterpreted. I was infuriated when it was clear a person writing to me did not bother to read my profile and was basing his interest solely on pictures of my ass. For instance, I stated no smokers, yet they smoked, or I stated I was not submissive and they were looking for a slave. They were superficial and just wanted to get fucked by anyone who would say yes.

Most emails were a simple "Hello" or "How are you?" I ignored those because they showed no effort. Some were outrageous offers to go on vacation or attend a party even though I had no idea who the sender was. I deleted those for obvious safety reasons. Others were filled with explicit sexual activities the sender wished to perform with me. Those irked me, as I was not a hooker. A few were extensive life stories and included details about the sender's job and hobbies. I disregarded those because the senders didn't grasp the point of the site. I responded mostly to messages that were direct yet respectful. For example, "I came across your profile and think I meet most of your requirements. I have been in the Lifestyle for several years and would love to take you out for a drink sometime to see if we are a match. Your pictures are fabulous! I have no problem driving to you. My face pics are open."

If I was looking for a new playmate I tended to do my own searches and reach out to the people I wanted to meet. It was more efficient than spending hours going through my inbox overflowing with terrible choices. I typically searched paid members with credits within a 50-mile radius who had been online within the past three days to confirm they were recently active and hopefully checking their messages frequently. I expected to meet within a week or two of initial contact. The sooner the better. Once two weeks passed my interest dropped, and I assumed they were playing games.

When I was not necessarily seeking new playmates (because I had enough regulars and no free time to spare) I checked my emails daily but only replied if there happened to be an exciting offer. I may have saved a screen name for later. I never responded to emails unless I was interested. I didn't have the patience to write "No, thank you" to hundreds of suitors. It was smart to have a list of extras in case I needed a last-minute replacement or suddenly had the urge for something different. I could take an eternity to get back to someone. I have honestly waited two years to reply to guys. They were shocked to hear from me out of the blue but still eager to meet. I was worth waiting two years for. Wow.

My standard procedure was to meet at a bar in my neighborhood. I rotated between a few places where I wouldn't hang out otherwise so bumping into a vanilla friend was not likely. Once or twice that happened, and I casually introduced my date by name and offered no further explanation. I was skilled at ending conversations quickly. It only seemed suspicious if we acted uncomfortable.

Once, however, I was at the gym and a woman I knew through other friends approached me. "Hey, were you at so-and-so bar last night?" she asked. I nodded. "I thought so, I was sitting next to you." Oh fuck! When I asked why she didn't say hello, she replied, "I didn't want to interrupt. You seemed to be enjoying a riveting conversation with your gentleman friend." OMG. My face turned red. My date and I were debating which was better—DV or DP. And in *explicit* detail. And knowing I get louder when I try to prove a point, I was sure she heard everything!

I wondered if the bartenders and wait staff recognized me and my constant flow of male companions. My designated bars were conveniently located within a mile of two hotels I frequented. I did not like meeting in hotel bars because I've learned it set the expectation we were definitely getting a room. I also did not reveal the name of the hotel until I decided we would wind up there because some guys pre-book the room which made rejecting them more offensive. One weekend I visited the same hotel Friday, Saturday and Sunday night. I hoped the front desk clerk didn't think I was an escort! I tended to drive myself to the hotel, so I could leave at any point. I never wanted to rely on the other person to get me home, and if the sex was terrible, getting in his car after was seriously tense! *Independence maintained control.*

This may sound funny, but I needed to carefully consider who I was fucking and when. A clever strategy allowed me to maximize my success. I didn't have sex just to have sex. I had sex to have *good* sex. Unknowns were tempting but unreliable. Regular guys were your favorite steak dish at your favorite restaurant whereas the new guy was the daily fish special on the menu. Would you be happily surprised with the fish or regret not sticking with your dependable steak? They could exceed expectations or totally fumble. The number of people that cancel last minute was astonishing. A date with a new person had a 50/50 chance of even happening so it was smart to schedule those in between

Chapter 8. Swinging Systems

regulars as a backup. However, with my regular guys, I evaluated what I was in for. Did we have sex for one hour or five? No, five hours was not an exaggeration! Did we have sex once or several times in one date? Were they sensual or aggressive? How rough were they? Did they want anal? How long did I need to recover in between them? Would the skin on my pussy be raw? Which guys could I fuck when I had my period? I get waxed, but a lot of guys shaved their genitals and the stubble could be irritating. Would my muscles be sore? My quads and forearms worked hard to support certain positions for extended periods. Fucking some of these guys was like a full contact sport or a high cardio workout.

Chapter 9

Grin and Bare It

Everyone has sex. It's a natural part of life. But how many people have *truly great, ultra quenching, completely fulfilling* sex? Close your eyes and envision your ultimate fantasy. How many people could say they thought it was easily attainable? I would bet not a lot. How many people just settle? That used to be me—but that was before I knew there were other alternatives. Swinging opened my eyes to a whole new world of possibilities and reprogrammed my brain to understand sex could be what I wanted it to be. There were no concrete rules and I could have sex purely for pleasure and not just for love.

I was apprehensive in the beginning. Generally, you have sex with a person you know. You build a rapport with him. You establish a level of comfort. Swinging is the complete opposite. It requires you to be bold up front. First impressions are crucial as they might be your one and only shot. I was way more judgmental about my behavior and my body than my partners were. I liked the idea of sex, but I was not actually comfortable in my own skin. I worried how I sounded when I moaned, how my face looked during an orgasm, how my pussy tasted. It was nerve wracking for sure! Here's the deal, though—anyone who was in bed with me wanted to be there. The guys I saw were attracted to me and they wanted me. They weren't disgusted by my physical imperfections. They adored every inch of me. I was the only one who was bothered by the fact that my thighs ever so slightly rubbed together. My partners thought my thick legs were sexy as hell. I worried my size D tits sagged too much without a bra, but they told me how luscious they were. I came to see myself through their eyes and finally realized, yeah, I should be proud of my body and I am desirable. Being confident gave me the ability to take sex from routine and mechanical to pleasurable and fun as hell!

Chapter 9. Grin and Bare It

News flash: You don't need to be a swinger to have great sex! Even if you are in a vanilla/monogamous relationship, you can improve your sex life by being more adventurous in small ways. To me, sex requires embracing all five senses. It should be messy; it should be organic and *mutually* rewarding.

1. Sight. We are visual creatures. Don't be scared to have sex with the lights on. The bed is your stage and you are the star. Don't worry how messed up your hair gets, or how the extra roll of fat on your stomach is magnified in certain positions, or if your make-up is smeared. Put a mirror next to the bed. Watching yourself/your partner from a different perspective is so hot. It is like you are a voyeur but you're watching yourself, your own porn. Open your eyes and make eye contact during sex for more passionate connections. Take pictures or videos to watch later.

    Or, if you are daring, incorporate a blindfold. Remove your sight and notice how your other senses intensify.

2. Taste. Good sex can get dirty, so enjoy it. Don't be grossed out if either of you is sweaty. Lick each other's body anyway. I know a lot of people that won't kiss after oral sex. This is a big disappointment for me. If your man is willing to put his mouth on your vagina, why won't you kiss him after? Why are you bothered by your own body? Kissing a guy after he goes down on me is so erotic. Or if he fingers me and then makes me lick his fingers. Suck his dick after he had been inside of you. All these things make for more intimacy.

3. Hearing. I used to be super quiet during sex and now I am one of the loudest people in the world during an orgasm. Don't be afraid to express your emotions verbally. Talk during sex, say deviant things whether you would do them in real life or not. This is fantasy time. Communicate during the act for better sex. If a guy is doing something you love, tell him. Encourage him to keep doing it. On the other hand, if he is not pleasing you, you need to tell him. You can be diplomatic and hint at something you like better or you can be straightforward and say you don't enjoy whatever he's doing. It is your body. Treat it kindly and get what you want out of sex. Help guide your partner to the

optimal way of giving you an orgasm. Some guys need a little help, which can involve trial and error, so communication is key. Remember, not speaking up is just promoting more bad sex. Ladies—*never* fake an orgasm. Don't make him think he is pleasing you if he is not. It is an injustice to yourself. And I just want to say that laughter and sex are also a good combo. Since sex should be fun, it is quite all right to laugh during it! A lot of mishaps can occur during a romp—you can't get your elaborate lingerie off, a dick slips in the wrong hole, someone falls off the bed, you get tangled in the sheets … just go with it!

4. Touch. This should be obvious, but get creative and learn what makes your partner go wild. Does he like to be touched gently on his face while you kiss? Does he go crazy if you gently tickle his balls during a blow job? Does he react if you pull his hair while he goes down on you? Do you intertwine your fingers with his? Do you want to play rough or soft? Does he pull your hair, slap you, choke you? Or maybe you switch it up and do those things to him! Does either of you have a spot on your body that sends chills up your spine when touched? Instead of having him cum inside you, let him cum on you—stomach, ass, face, however kinky you are feeling. Feeling warm cum on my body turns me on. Either you clean it up with a towel or he rubs it all over you—maybe, if he is extra nasty, he licks it up (yes, that is a possibility). You have options. Test out lotions and oils to make things slippery. Keep fucking your guy after he cums. Not all guys can stay hard, but if he can, continue a few more minutes. His body will be extra sensitive.

5. Smell. Face it: Sex has a smell. Sometimes good, sometimes bad, but it comes with the territory. Everyone's bodies and genitals smell different especially when we sweat; get turned on and cum. Don't worry. You two can shower together after!

Most important, sex should be honest—with your partner, obviously, but with yourself as well. Be bold. Discuss sex over a few beers. Get to know one another's likes and dislikes. Have fun. Make a list of things you want to try!

Chapter 9. Grin and Bare It

Squirting

Before swinging I didn't know what squirting was. I never watched porn. I was naïve. Now squirting is my favorite! When I started swinging there was a lot of talk about squirting; it was mentioned in a lot of profiles. Apparently, a lot of Lifestyle guys are experts at it. People would ask me if I could do it and I would reply no. Oh, was I wrong! I'm still not sure how or why it happens, but now the answer is yes, I can—and please make me do it!

My first squirting experience happened when I was with a couple. The husband put his fingers inside me and suddenly I screamed because I thought I peed the couch. When I looked at him he was smiling from ear to ear. He saw me panic for a moment and said, "Calm down, you're just squirting—enjoy it!" A few minutes later I stood up and the entire couch was soaked. I was shocked. Squirting was amazing! An unrivaled sensation.

Several guys could make me squirt on command while others were unsuccessful. With the right technique, I could drench the guy's shirt or sleeve, his face, my face. I could flood the entire bed. It was uncontrollable, as if someone opened a fire hydrant. This party trick is simultaneously erotic and funny. It was always a good performance at a club and left people in awe of my abilities.

While I am very squirt-friendly with hands, I have only ever squirted during intercourse with one guy, Peter. We were longtime partners who always had amazing sex. He was exasperated because as hard as he tried he couldn't get my body to do squirt with his hands. I was on top of him as usual when a gush of liquid sprayed everywhere, all over his chest and face. I froze, mortified. I looked down at him and he grinned so wide—then laughed hysterically and high-fived me. He thought it was the hottest thing ever. Guys love squirting! It happened a few more times with him but never with anyone else. Who knows why?

For me, the key is relaxing—mentally and physically. It doesn't work if I overthink it. Training your body can be tricky because during an orgasm your muscles naturally tense and tighten but you need to loosen up and let go to allow the magic to happen. Some guys will literally tell me to unclench because they can feel the tension with their hands. Understanding my body took a bit of practice, but I am pretty good at it now! Also, I need to be properly hydrated beforehand. I can lose so much fluid during repeated squirting episodes that it almost cripples me (in a good way, of course).

I was at a party and my date basically used me to hold an educational seminar to teach guys the magic touch. They took turns as he critiqued their technique. I found this hysterical, but my friend nonchalantly replied, "How else are they gonna learn? You have to share your knowledge." I thought that was very cool of him and the guys absolutely appreciated our tutorial. Squirting is something every woman should experience. Don't be afraid to mention it to your man. It's undoubtedly an art form to be studied like cake decorating or sushi rolling. Watch a YouTube video and practice together!

Toys

I grew up sexually repressed. I never masturbated, which people find hard to grasp because I am so sexual now. I always thought toys were for lonely girls who couldn't get laid. I saw masturbating as depressing instead of empowering. I was uncomfortable touching myself and thought it was an embarrassing topic of discussion, but I was just uneducated. Every part of swinging was intriguing, and I wanted to try every experience to judge it for myself. I still never masturbate—but only because I have so much sex I never need to. However, I am totally a fan of using toys in the bedroom. I knew toys could be used solitary, but I learned they were even better with a partner. They added another level of intensity to sex. Fucking a guy while you hold a vibrator on your clit is marvelous. Maybe he controlled the toy or maybe I did, which also changed the sensation. Wear a butt plug while you get fucked vaginally or use a dildo vaginally while he fucks you in the ass. Or insert a vibrator in your pussy along with his dick. These are all wonderfully pleasurable options. Toys can be interactive and fun. Using them can bring you and your partner closer and rev up your sex life. You can simulate the physical feeling of fucking multiple partners without having to literally add another person.

Anal

I had a bad experience years ago with Elliot and never thought I'd become an anal girl. I just thought it was unnecessary pain and seemed too personal due to the potential mess factor. Anal was not an option and then I met Luis (who I will introduce you to later) and he guided me through it properly. I honestly couldn't believe how easy it was.

First step was being comfortable together, relaxing. He started with a finger in my ass during intercourse then we moved to a small butt plug, then a larger one, then eventually his cock. He always made sure I was extremely turned on and wet before we tried. I would get on all fours and I would back my ass into him. He said I had the control. I went at my pace. Once he was in all the way, he started slowly, then OMG the pounding I could take! I had no idea! I was impressed with myself. Gold star! I don't generally crave anal, but I do enjoy it occasionally in the right situation, especially with two guys. DP (double penetration) is fucking hot and the combination of the cock in your vagina makes the one in your ass more pleasurable. I somewhat prefer DP to just anal.

Anal was reserved for special guys and occasions. I had to mentally and physically prepare. I was terrified of having a bad anal experience, so I would watch my diet and refrain from certain foods. Shitting on someone was my worst nightmare. How do you recover from that? I was so paranoid of having an accident that I would ritually try so hard to go to the bathroom before I left my house. Eating yogurt usually helped. If my stomach ever felt questionable, I would eat a peanut butter sandwich, hoping to create some blockage. Luckily, I never had an issue! My system worked. I have heard girls who prefer anal go so far as to have enemas or take Imodium before their dates. One guy told me he performed double anal on a girl. Yes, double, as in two cocks in one asshole! Are you kidding me? I can never imagine that.

Chapter 10

My Swinging BFF

I met Max, short for Maximillian, early on. He was Polish, had a fit body, and was in his late 40s and was a veteran swinger. He worked a 9-to-5 job as a dentist, but on weekends he fucked as many women as he could. He was bawdy and spoke about sex so naturally, like he was talking about sports or movies. Max was famous for getting blow jobs in his car and having women lick his asshole. He often attended small orgies and hung out at a swingers bar. When I met him at that bar we would compete to see who had fucked more of the people who were there. Max and I shared a distaste for those who wouldn't play on a first date or needed to hang out and bond for hours before agreeing to fuck. Amateurs. We wanted to fuck as fast as we could, and, if it was early enough, maybe fuck someone else. He became my swinging BFF and we loved to gossip and share stories of our dates. We would text each other updates all hours of the night or call and describe every single detail. Nothing was sacred and the more graphic the better. He fucked so many people I joked he was a celebrity and cumming on a girl's face was his autograph. I guess now that he is in a book, he is famous! We lived far apart and only had sex a few times, but our friendship was solid.

On our first date Max got out of the car, and when he said hello, he kissed me—tongue and all. I thought, "Wow, this guy is bold." We had dinner and I had to read him the menu because he forgot his glasses. Our hotel room turned out to be the most bizarre thing ever. It was a small room with a tiny twin bed and a nightstand holding a lamp. The bathroom was communal at the end of the hall. It was strange, but it didn't stop us from having fun. Our sex was good, but it was purely physical, not passionate, and he was honorable, a trait seldom found among single guys. He was a prime example of a true Lifestyle guy.

Chapter 10. My Swinging BFF

Max and I attended a few parties together but never actually full swapped successfully.

I was his date for a hotel takeover, when a host rents a section of a hotel and hundreds of swingers attend. We drove separately, and I arrived first. I was in my work clothes carrying my duffle bag filled with sexy clothes. I thought I had the wrong place because the lobby was filled with Hassidic Jews. I thought that was strange, so I called Max and he confirmed the address. He soon walked in and was equally as baffled. It just didn't seem to be the appropriate crowd for a takeover. He checked in and we were directed to the other wing of the hotel which made a little more sense. We chilled in our room on the fifth floor and caught up about our recent affairs, compared stories. We had sex and then went to the shower. We are both intelligent yet could not for the life of us turn on the water. There was no handle or knob, so Max called the front desk and we waited for help. The maintenance guy revealed a well-hidden button underneath the faucet and assured us everyone needed help finding it. This night was weird already. I wore tight white capris and a white lacy bra as a top and gold sandals. We headed to the sixth floor for the pre-party meet and greet. One room was used as the check in and we gave our names and received wrist bands. The rest of the rooms on that floor and the floors above and below were also occupied by swingers. All the doors were wide open, and people congregated in the hallways, sauntering in and out of rooms, mingling. It reminded me of a college dorm.

At 7 the main ballroom opened so a large group of us crammed in the elevator and headed down. On the third floor the doors opened, and a Jewish father and his young sons stepped on. Awkward-central! He refused to make eye contact with us and gazed at the floor. I was in my bra top, cleavage exposed. Another woman was wearing a see-through dress and another had on an outfit with so many slits and openings it looked like she had been attacked with a razor blade. I couldn't figure out how it even stayed on her body. The little boys were mesmerized and stared at us with wide eyes. One woman said to me, "I love your tits, can I feel them?" I said, "Sure." She cupped one breast in each hand. You could feel the uncomfortable energy and I was mortified. The doors opened at the lobby and the Jewish father couldn't get his family out fast enough. The rest of us paused and shared a good laugh.

The dance floor was congested, and the room was full. Max and I inventoried the crowd. Older than we expected and not very attractive according to our preferences. We attempted to be social, but dancing seemed like a waste of time when sex was an option, and a lot of the people were cliquey, sticking to their own group of friends.

We judged everyone's outfits and rated their looks and dance skills. Sex was not allowed here so the dance floor became a place for foreplay—grinding bodies and clusters of women making out and revealing their tits. One woman had someone's hand up her skirt, getting fingered. Max and I were bored. The music continued until midnight and by then we were both tired and losing interest. These parties were all about socializing and we were not. The crowd finally flocked upstairs, and the halls were flooded with rowdy people. A DJ was blasting more tunes. We scoped out the scene in different rooms with little interest. We headed to our room and fucked, then wandered the halls again. A few guys were getting blow jobs and some couples were having sex, but nothing overly exciting. It was not the graphic orgy we expected so we went to bed. I only went to one other hotel takeover after that and it was the same deal. I decided they are just not for me although most people find them awesome.

Max and I hardly ever saw each other due to the distance but we kept in touch. He was still the first person I called when I needed to complain or share a laugh over a preposterous story.

Chapter 11

Psycho Swinger

As previously stated, the cardinal rule in swinging is no attachment. When I was with my ex-boyfriend it wasn't relevant. I had him, I loved him. Other people were mere objects, human sex toys for our pleasure. As a single girl, couples were never an issue from my perspective because it was pure fantasy. I was an object for them, a novelty item, a guest star on a TV show.

Most guys were NSA. I saw them once or a few times and it was strictly sex. Dates progressed efficiently—meet in public for a drink, feel safe, go fuck. Be done in an hour or two. There was little to no communication in between sessions and we never discussed much about our personal lives beyond first names and the towns we lived in. It was NSA without a doubt. I remained detached and forgot them the next day. However, I am naturally an emotional person, a relationship person, a warm person, so the first single guy that became a long-term steady playmate got tragically messy for me. That was another negative side effect of being single.

With much regret, I admit that in my early days I did in fact fall victim to the detested "crazy girl" syndrome. It was hard to keep that clear distinction because we blurred the line between swinging and vanilla, sex and intimacy. We were highly compatible. Simple fuck sessions morphed into all night hangout events. The more we had sex, the more personal it got, the closer the bond became. I got confused. I swore he was my soul mate. It was agony. I guess I was at fault for getting carried away, but that didn't make the pain any easier to accept.

Anyone who met me later in my swinging career would probably be shocked by this story because I am now so cool and collected. I almost didn't include this because it was so humiliating, but since it deeply affected me, it seemed crucial to add.

Peter sent me an email stating he lived 45 minutes away but conveniently worked in my neighborhood. He was a pharmaceutical rep, early 40s and so fucking hot. When I read his message, I stared at his photos in disbelief. I knew being a Unicorn made me a hot commodity, but I thought he was way out of my league. I ardently replied to him and I suggested we text because it was a faster way to communicate. Peter contacted me, and I was drawn to him instantly. Our conversation began purely vanilla. We shared basic information like our jobs, our hobbies, how and why we ended up on the site and so on. We shared the same witty sense of humor and appreciated cutting sarcasm. Within a few hours we gradually started discussing our sexual preferences, our likes and dislikes. Apparently, we both favored rough, passionate, sweaty, animalistic sex. He told me I had a flawless body and he was dying to touch me and taste me. We began flirting heavily over the next few days. We texted for hours at a stretch. We desperately wanted to meet in person, but I inconveniently had my period. We considered just meeting for a drink with no intention of fucking, but we agreed that would be torturous. It would take way too much self-control not to rip each other's clothes off, so we figured it was best to wait a few days until my period was gone and we could meet with no limitations. In the meantime, we continued to talk constantly. The anticipation was building with every word, like a water balloon expanding to its max.

Normally I preferred to remain local, but I had literally just moved to a new apartment the day before we planned to meet and of course my new bed had not been delivered yet! I wanted to meet him so badly I offered to make the short drive to his area. I had no doubt it would be worth it.

We met at a sports bar. I wore the sexiest outfit I could find in my closet—a short red skin-tight dress that was low cut in front giving me excessive cleavage. When I walked it would get shorter with every step, so I had to keep puling it down. I scanned the bar but did not see Peter, so I headed straight for the restroom. I always needed to pee when I was nervous. I adjusted my dress in the mirror once more and reapplied my lip gloss. My phone vibrated, and the text said, "I am here. I think you walked right by me." I replied, "I'll be right there."

I exited the restroom and surveyed the tables surrounding the bar. It was moderately crowded, but the one table was occupied by a single

Chapter 11. Psycho Swinger

male. There he was. He looked up from the menu as I approached. He smiled and stood up. He was very preppy, wearing a light pink polo shirt and khakis. He was tall and fit. I could tell he was no stranger to the gym. He was Norwegian, with brownish blond hair and green eyes, dimples, and the brightest white teeth I have ever seen. He looked like he could've been in a boy band or a toothpaste commercial. I usually preferred dark hair and eyes, but he was an exception I was happy to make. He was the type of guy you wanted to show up at a high school reunion with to make the other girls envious. We exchanged an awkward hello as we couldn't decide if we should hug or kiss. So smooth, I thought to myself.

We sat down and ordered beers and appetizers. I was so jittery I couldn't eat. He was just so handsome I still couldn't accept the fact that he wanted to meet me. I imagined he was used to fucking models and beauty pageant contestants. After a rocky start, I started to unwind, and the conversation became natural. It was just like our texts had been, fun and easy. We chilled there for an hour or so. Peter paid the tab and I was prepared to go home. We had a great time, but I didn't sense the sexual attraction from him I was hoping for.

As we walked toward the front door he complimented my boots. A small victory. Then he complimented my ass. Now I thought there may be some hope. He was behind me as we weaved through the dark parking lot. I pointed to a car: "That's mine." When I was a few feet away from my car I felt a hand on my ass. I quickly spun around, and Peter's face was directly in front of mine. He grabbed me by the back of the head, his fingers in my hair, and he kissed me! The kiss was so good I practically melted. A splendid combination of dominance and passion. He let me go and said, "I think you should come back to my place." I normally did not go to strangers' apartments on a first date due to obvious safety concerns, but I said "Yes" without any hesitation. He kissed me again. "I live a few blocks away, just follow me." I tried to sound cool when I replied, "Sure, no problem." I hopped in my car, and with the windows up and radio on, I let out a scream of pure joy.

A few traffic lights later we both pulled in at his place. He lived in ranch style house in a nice neighborhood. The landscaped lawn looked expensive. I followed him down the walkway and up the cement steps without saying a word. Peter unlocked the door and moved aside so I could enter first. What a gentleman. I heard the door shut behind me, and without any warning, he pushed me against the wall. One hand grabbed my neck while he shoved his tongue in my mouth. His other hand was between my legs. I guess the gentleman turned into a beast. It was so sexy. I was so wet as his hand snuck under my panties. He pulled his lips away from mine and dropped to his knees. He frantically lifted my dress and pushed my lace panties to one side. His mouth was all over me. I closed my eyes and my legs weakened. All the fantasies we discussed via text were coming to life.

A few moments later he stood up, grabbed my hand and pushed me toward the bedroom. He pulled my dress off over my head and threw me onto his king-size bed. His shirt came off and he was on top of me. We were kissing and grabbing at each other. Next his pants disappeared and suddenly his rock-hard dick was inside me. No time for condoms. His entering me was an unbeatable feeling. He fucked me so hard and I screamed so loud. We switched, and I fucked him while he pulled my hair. We were both sweating and gasping for air.

We had to stop and take a break for a minute. He flipped the air conditioner on, put music on and retrieved a few bottles of water from the fridge. I confessed I didn't think we were going to have sex. "Why not?" he asked. I admitted I didn't think he was attracted to me at the bar. Peter laughed. "It took all of my might not to reach across the table and fuck you right in the bar." I was beaming! We had another round of crazy hot sex before I went home. At that point, he had been, without a doubt, the best sex since I joined the site—maybe in my entire life.

I texted him when I got home to reiterate what a phenomenal time I had. The next morning our texts relived the previous night and we both agreed we needed to do that again—and soon! The next week I went back to his house. He ordered dinner for us and we sat on the oversized L-shaped couch and watched TV as we ate and talked. He felt like an old friend. Like we had known each other for years. I was impressed with his décor. For a single guy, he had impeccable taste. Eventually we moved to the bedroom. He lowered the lights and turned on music and we fucked for several hours. We were so compatible. Every kiss, every touch was magnificent. Every movement was in sync. It was hard to believe sex with a stranger could be so perfect. The chemistry was amazing. And this meeting was even better than the first.

Chapter 11. Psycho Swinger 87

Peter and I became weekly playmates. Our routine was dinner, gossip and sex. Peter was fascinated how my experiences as a single girl were so different than his. He marveled at how many emails I got and how many people I was able to easily meet. He thoroughly enjoyed hearing my stories and especially got a kick out of my bad dates. I spent seven or eight hours at his place at a stretch. We shared a lot of good laughs. In the bedroom, we fucked for a few hours then listened to music during our breaks. We sipped wine and compared recent songs we discovered. We tackled crossword puzzles or read our horoscopes. We chatted about our families and friends and got wrapped up in deep discussions about life and relationships. Debated the pros and cons of dating vanilla versus being in the Lifestyle.

My relationship with Peter was convoluted. He was my first consistent friend with benefits. Before I met him, my affairs were black and white, but this was different—we were in the gray zone. After several months, I started to develop real feelings for him. He openly discussed that he wanted a girlfriend. One night he even asked my opinion of his Match.com profile. As I read it I couldn't help but think to myself I was his ideal mate. His description of the perfect girl was me. He wanted a girl who listened to Reggae music. Check. A girl who was comfortable getting dressed up for a night on the town or comfortable curled up on the couch in his old t-shirt. I just so happened to be on his couch wearing his college sweatshirt as I read this. Check. A girl who adored family and friends, was ambitious and appreciated sarcasm. Triple check. The list continued, and I met every requirement. Did he show me this profile because he was trying to tell me he wanted me? I thought so!

Dating seemed like the obvious solution to me. We both missed being in a relationship and we clearly had great sexual chemistry. Our family lives were similar. We were both highly sexual and enjoyed swinging. He repeatedly told me I was the best sex he ever had. Couldn't get any better. There was only one small problem. Peter only wanted to date a vanilla girl. I couldn't understand why. We had talked about it before and I heard what he said, but it didn't make any sense. A vanilla girl would never satisfy him long term. He loved the Lifestyle too much. The thrill and the sexiness. He needed a girl like me; he just didn't know it.

A few more months passed, and our bond became stronger. We

ventured out to a club and a few parties together. Acting as a couple felt so right. The way we looked at each other, the way we touched. Even other people could see it! They automatically assumed we were a real couple. That solidified my belief we were meant to be together. We were still both fucking other people, but it was only a matter of time before he woke up and asked me to be his girlfriend. At least that's what happened in my mind.

Separating the sex from my emotions became increasingly difficult. My head was spinning trying to decide how to define our relationship. I invited him to grab a drink after work, so we went to a barbecue joint in my neighborhood that was empty except for us. We sat at the bar in the corner facing each other. After a few drinks, I admitted I had developed feelings for him. Peter said he hadn't for me. I told him I was concerned because we were falling into a dangerous hazy area where we were labeled NSA but acted like boyfriend and girlfriend. That he missed being in a relationship was no secret. I suspected he was projecting that onto me. I admitted it was painful for me. At first, he denied it but finally he accepted that his behavior was misleading. He agreed to tone it down and act less intimate and affectionate. We did not have sex that night. It just didn't feel right.

A few weeks later we were hanging out as we always did. A typical night. After we fucked, Peter casually asked me if I wanted to see a video of him fucking a housewife he met. I cringed. "No, I don't," I replied. I was offended. I abruptly told him I needed to go. I got dressed and stormed out. Later that night I called him and told him I cared for him, and his comment pissed me off because I was jealous. He acted so surprised. I told him it still felt like we were perpetually stuck in limbo. In fact, I wanted to date. Unfortunately, Peter did not share my sentiments. He maintained that this was just sex. We were friends with benefits in its truest form. I disagreed. There was emotion involved here. The way he looked at me, the way he held my hand when he fucked me, the way he kissed me. It was not just sex. I'm a girl who fucked a lot of guys. I could tell the difference. We got into a huge argument and I told Peter I was done with him. I never wanted to see him again. I accused him of being a selfish asshole who was too blind to see what was right in front of him.

Peter obeyed my wishes and I never heard from him. After a few

Chapter 11. Psycho Swinger

days of silence, I was even more enraged. Who the fuck does he think he is? How could he not apologize for being a douchebag? How could he not realize I was his dream girl? I was in panic mode. The thought of never seeing him again made it hard to breathe. To make matters worse I couldn't talk to any of my friends because he didn't exist in my real world. The voices in my head were competing. One told me to let him go. He was not worth the time or effort if he didn't appreciate me. However, the other voice was more powerful. It demanded I get him to admit he loved me. I was willing to help guide him to enlightenment. I was willing to give him another chance to mend our relationship. So I finally texted him. I apologized and said I missed him. He said he missed me too. I knew it! He was probably ecstatic that I reached out to him.

We texted back and forth and made a date to hang out. I went to his house and we immediately fell right back into our routine. As we laid in bed cuddling after sex I couldn't resist bringing up our fight. I never could keep my mouth shut. I just needed him to validate my feelings. Again, he firmly stated this was just sex. It was nothing more and never would be. From then on, I lost my mind. Our new routine became hanging out a few times, peacefully, then I would randomly explode and tell him I couldn't handle this NSA bullshit and we were through. Eventually, I called him and we picked up where we left off. It was unhealthy. Once I deleted his phone number in a fit of rage, then I had to email him and ask for his number. He could've not answered me or told me he didn't want to hang out. He was sending mixed signals.

We had been on a hiatus for about a month. I thought about him constantly. I hoped time apart would cure me, but it didn't. I just wanted him more. His rejection was a scab I couldn't stop picking at no matter how hard I tried.

By a stroke of sheer luck, I was caller 100 on a radio station and won tickets to a two-day Reggae festival. I threw my hands in the air and shouted. I was so psyched!

None of my friends were Reggae fans but I immediately knew who was. Peter. We spent countless hours listening to our favorite songs and we were both equally passionate about it. We hadn't been in touch for more than a month, but he was my ideal date. For days I contemplated whether I should invite him. Why couldn't I get over this guy? I was obsessed. I couldn't accept that I gave so much of myself to someone who took it with no remorse. Maybe this was similar to what I felt with Elliot. If he left his wife the suffering would have been worth it. If Peter finally said he loved me then my efforts were worth it. I would be validated. Clearly, I had not mastered the art of solo swinging yet!

I typed and deleted several messages to Peter before I had the nerve to hit send. I paced my living room. This was a major decision. My willpower finally collapsed, and I sent him a "What's up, stranger?" text with a smiley emoji. As soon as it entered the digital universe I panicked. What if he didn't respond? Why am I so pathetic? Almost immediately my phone beeped, and I saw an incoming text from him. I let out a massive breath. He does care.

Our conversation flowed surprisingly easily, like all our previous issues never existed. That was another reason I couldn't sever the cord. The fact that he always welcomed me back into his life gave me false encouragement.

I told him I'd won tickets to a two-day Reggae festival and I could tell I had his attention. "Who are you taking?" "I'm not sure yet," I responded. "I love Reggae," he added. "Would you go if I invited you?" I asked casually. "You have to ask me to find out," he replied. So annoying. A vexing game of cat and mouse ensued. "Are you just trying to trick me into asking you just so you can say no?" "Only one way to find out," he said. God, I hated him. And I hated myself for not actually hating him at all. I bit my lip and texted, "Peter, I am cordially inviting you to attend the Reggae Fest on Saturday May 20th." A long pause followed and my blood boiled. That mother fucker was going to say no. After an eternity, my phone beeped, and I opened his message while holding my breath. It said "YES! I would love to." Capital letters and exclamation point. Wow! He does miss me. Am I psychotic or what?

Peter was so excited that he immediately turned into a serious event planner. Since the festival was two hours away, he was going to book a room so we could spend the night there. He oozed enthusiasm. In all the months I knew him I never saw him put so much effort into hanging out. Maybe this was going to be the magical weekend that would lead to our eternal happiness together.

The concert was two weeks away and we were both amped. We texted constantly, the anticipation building. When the big day arrived,

Chapter 11. Psycho Swinger

Peter picked me up at 2 in the afternoon at my apartment. I waited on the curb with my little suitcase like a kid waiting for the bus on the first day of school. A shiny silver Lexus RX 350 pulled up in front of me. He had gotten a new car since I had seen him last. The driver side door opened, and he was as gorgeous as I remembered. His smile was wide as he gave me a huge hug. Peter was talking a mile a minute as he put my bag in the trunk. He was as merry as a kid on Christmas morning. Was it because of me or the festival? Didn't matter. We hopped in the car and we were off. We had a few sarcastic exchanges about me hating him and him being a dick, then the tension evaporated. Tunes blasted, my hair blew in the breeze from the open sun roof and his hand was on my knee. What could be better?

At 4:15 we arrived at our hotel. Peter parked the car and checked us in at the front desk. Our room was spacious with a king-size bed and a seating area with a large sofa and coffee table. We both showered. As I dried my hair I watched his reflection in the mirror as he planned what to wear. I laughed. It was adorable that this 40-year-old guy was so indecisive about his outfit. He spread out on the bed the multiple shirts and hats he packed for the night. I brought one dress. It was the dress I wore the first night I met him. I thought it was romantic. I chose a red hat and a t-shirt with an American flag on the front, handed it to him, and said, "Move it, buddy."

We held hands as we exited the elevator into the main lobby. Being with him, appearing to be a loving couple, felt good. We found a bar with two empty seats and got cozy. It was an all–American burger-type place with several beers on tap. We ordered two Stellas and said "Cheers" as we clinked glasses. The bartender handed us a menu to share and we settled on burgers—his with a fried egg, mine with avocado. We added an order of cheese fries and onion rings. Fuck it. This was a special night; let's live it up. Our food was followed by one more beer we had to gulp down fast because the show began in 15 minutes. Time always flew when we were together.

We sat in the second to last row of the arena but we still had a perfect view of the stage. Peter had his arm around my shoulder the entire night except for when he needed his hand to videotape his favorite songs being performed. I enjoyed seeing him so cheerful. This had to earn me points! When bands we knew were singing, we shouted the lyrics along with them. When unfamiliar artists were on stage, we rated their songs.

The events ended around 11 so we moseyed back to our room figuring we could find other ways to entertain ourselves. Peter escorted me to the bed and kissed me as we undressed each other. He laid me down and leaned over me as he slid his cock into me. He fucked me for a while and something seemed off. I decided I should get on top. That always turned me on and guaranteed a ton of orgasms. As I rode him it still felt different. After the time and energy that I spent chasing him, I didn't enjoy the sex. How interesting this was. And confusing! Our sex only lasted about 30 minutes compared to three or four hours because we were so tired. He passed out on the plush white comforter and I retreated to the couch. I barely slept because my mind was trying to process my emotions.

The next morning, we scanned the room for any belongings we forgot to pack and turned off the lights as we left. I was quiet. We capitalized on the elaborate complimentary breakfast buffet and headed out to the festival. It was fun, but I was more reserved. At 7 we made one more restroom stop before we hit the road. We listened to the CDs he bought at the souvenir booth. I barely spoke. I was itching to get home, which was odd. I usually never wanted to leave him.

We saw each other a few more times in the following months but it was never the same. Something died inside me. Or maybe the opposite happened. Maybe I became alive when I realized I deserved more. I was too tired of endlessly giving myself to someone who did not appreciate it. I haven't had contact with him in more than a year.

We ended on terrible terms. He never told me why he didn't want to date me and not having closure tormented me. Those ten months with Peter taught me a lot of lessons. He was a pivotal person and not the most shining moment of my swinging career.

I think one of the biggest problems I encountered was I had no frame of reference and no one to guide me. I had female vanilla friends who could sympathize with heartbreak and douchebag guys, but I couldn't discuss Peter because they didn't know I was in the Lifestyle, so I couldn't fully explain the situation. They wouldn't understand anyway. My Lifestyle male friends tried to give me advice, but they couldn't relate to my feminine emotions. Even the married Lifestyle women were clueless about my dilemma because they were happily married and never got attached to other people they played with. I felt so alone. Keeping everything bottled up inside drove me insane. After Peter, I became much more guarded and taught myself to separate emotions from the physical part of sex. That lesson was the silver lining, I guess. He saved me from many future heartbreaks.

Chapter 12

Socks and Soup

Single guys—boy, did they have it tough! Unlike Unicorns, single guys were an oversaturated market. There were so many of them it was insane. They were not all created equal and sifting through them was time-consuming. Here are a couple of tips for any novice swingers. (1) Show up. (2) Don't be a douchebag. Sounds reasonable, right?

I categorized single guys into three columns: those just trying to get laid (the majority), those attempting to enter the Lifestyle, and true Lifestylers—and distinguishing them is easy for me *now*. Assholes seeking quick, easy sex were the reason single guys got a bad reputation. They immediately start with lewd e-mails and send a lot of unrequested dick pics. They do not take no for an answer and hound me incessantly. They ask what I will do for them, do not care who I am as a person and assume that meeting me for a drink guarantees I will fuck them. I am a living, breathing sex doll to them. They are disrespectful, lazy, feel entitled and do not want to put forth any effort. They complain about traveling or won't spend the money to get a room. They are selfish in bed and their orgasm is the priority. They act like they deserve me and are ignorant to the fact that there is more to this process than the physical act of penetration. Desperate guys are referred to as "thirsty."

Inexperienced guys getting acclimated to the Lifestyle could be problematic. They think they understand the world they are entering but have no practical experience. Half were so overly confident, talking a big game and making promises they could not fulfill. The other half were too nervous to make a move. Usually, in both cases, the pressure got to them and they couldn't even get an erection. Having sex on command could be intimidating! Especially when they met an alpha female.

Often, they misunderstand the nuances. For example, I met a first

Chapter 12. Socks and Soup

timer and we went out to dinner on three separate occasions. On the third night, I asked him why we hadn't have sex yet. He replied that I was a nice girl and he didn't want to offend me by pressuring me for sex. As endearing as that was, I kindly reminded him we met on a sex site and I wanted to get fucked. This revelation thrilled him, so we went to a hotel and he could not get hard. He confessed having sex with a stranger was unnatural. I gave him a pep talk and advised him he needed to put up or shut up in this world. It's easier said than done. Countless times I met new guys for drinks, and when I asked if they were ready to get a room, they looked like a deer in the headlights. "You mean right now?" Another new guy covered the hotel room in rose petals. He thought he hit the nail on the head in the romance department and I was taken aback. I reminded him this was NSA sex, not a honeymoon. Eventually I stopped meeting newbies because I didn't enjoy having to be the conductor.

On the other hand, real Lifestyle guys were wonderful. They were the needle in the haystack. The majority had experience being part of a couple so were more mindful. They genuinely appreciated the fact I was allowing them to enjoy me. They were all about respect, always behaving as gentlemen. They asked what they could do for me, what my turn-ons were. They met me understanding there were no expectations and accepted that no means no without being offended. Their primary focus was my pleasure. These guys could be separated into two further sub-categories: those who want to and those who can. The first group means well but falls short somehow. They are lovely people and have a Lifestyle mentality but maybe they aren't as skilled, or have poor stamina, or can't perform under pressure, or just can't match my style. The second was the ultimate score. The difference between the two groups was like having a GED versus a Ph.D. in sex. Or owning a power tool versus knowing how to use it to build a house. Guys in the second group have been in every situation so have extensive knowledge and hands-on experience. They were very skilled sexually, could read my body better than I could and taught me things I didn't know. They were secure and never pushy. They came prepared with a plethora of toys, the ability to switch gears and innovative positions.

Single guys have limited access to parties and events. They are only allowed on certain nights and pay a high fee to get in. Often, they pick up the bar/hotel bill or split it with couples, they always pay for girls, and they should do the travelling. I often wonder how much money they spend per year on swinging. It must be expensive as hell! I guess it is an investment just as any other hobby.

Guys can be straight or bi, and a few are trans. Some are very jealous, and we never discuss our other sexual activities. Others love to share stories and compare notes and offer advice. Then there are those who love to know what I'm doing because it gets them off. They want to fuck me after another guy does, sometimes only after, and they want to see videos and pictures.

When it came to single guys I could play one on one, meaning just the two of us, or there could be group play, meaning me and multiple guys.

One-night stands/NSA sex required physical chemistry and not much else. Think of NSA partners as a pair of socks. You understood they were functional. They served a purpose and kept your feet warm. If you lost one in the dryer you might be momentarily bummed but it held no sentimental value and could easily be replaced. You buy a new pair and forget about the old one. You moved on quickly.

I always tried to have a few regular playmates, which I called "my stable." They would be categorized as FWB (friends with benefits). In addition to chemistry there needed to be substance. We were compatible sexually as well as in terms of personality. Pretend FWB were like soup—hearty, warm and filling. They nourished you. One guy was a bowl of chicken noodle soup—he always made you feel good. But occasionally you had an urge for something spicier, so you ordered a cup of Thai chili. Enjoying the Thai chili doesn't negate how much you still enjoy the chicken noodle. Maybe another day you wanted something creamier, so you got chowder. There were so many flavors and each one satisfied a distinct craving. If you spilled your soup, you were sad because your bowl was empty. You couldn't snap your fingers and instantly have more soup. Buying groceries, preparing ingredients and cooking it took time. FWB were separate entities, not interchangeable cocks. They rotated depending on our schedules and my mood. I may have seen them often, occasionally or infrequently, but we always kept in touch via phone calls or texts. We checked in to discuss our jobs and families, bitch about bad days, share good news, or maybe just to say we were thinking of each other.

Chapter 12. Socks and Soup

Following Peter, I had a few more situations where consistent playdates with guys lead to incredibly close bonds and mixed in vanilla activities. There was a level of comfort which led to more passionate sex. We spent so much time together, having sex could be more reminiscent of making love. The way we touched, how we cuddled afterward. It had some qualities of a relationship, but it wasn't. I constantly reminded myself this was just swinging. I did not want another crazy girl relapse! I knew there were no expectations of exclusivity or love. We shared the affection we craved without any responsibility or commitment. This eliminated my need for vanilla dates.

Involvement lasted anywhere from months to years and intensity levels varied. Each guy was so different, and I received something specific I was lacking from each.

Vincenzo (NSA with Prescheduled Dates)

I met Vincenzo at a bar on a Monday afternoon. He had wanted to meet me for almost a year. He was Sicilian, only a few inches taller than me, and he had wavy black hair that made him look overdue for a haircut. He was on the quiet and reserved side, but after a drink he asked me to the hotel and I said yes. The receptionist wouldn't let him use his credit card because he didn't have his ID, so Vincenzo asked if I would mind using my card and said he would give me cash. Against my better judgment I agreed as he went to find an ATM. The woman informed me it would be $498 and I asked her to repeat that. I called Vincenzo and asked if he was aware of the pricey rate and he said yes. I thought that was a steep price tag no matter how good the sex was. He returned and as we went to the room I wondered when he was going to hand over the money.

We sat on the king-sized bed with a floral comforter and started to make out. Things were heating up, but I was distracted, hoping I wasn't just being tricked into paying the bill. Vincenzo removed his shirt and he was athletic with a thin strip of neatly manicured hair trailing down his stomach. Then he became an animal. The sex was rough and intense. He bent me over and wrapped a towel around my waist so he could fuck me deep and hard and I couldn't resist him. When he was on top of me his sweat dripped onto my face and chest. It was sexy and messy and our bodies became a slip and slide. After a few hours, we collapsed on the bed and I exclaimed, "I sure wasn't expecting that." He smiled and said, "I like to take people by surprise." As we tried to catch our breath we chatted and discovered we both loved movies and had the same taste in obscure films. Before he left he placed cash on the nightstand and I was relieved to know he was a man of his word.

Vincenzo and I became regular partners. We rotated between going to movie matinees (he had a weak spot for Sour Patch Kids) and fucking. I found a much cheaper hotel and the routine was I would get the room and he would bring Gatorade and leave cash before he departed. We were there so often the hostess knew me by name. After sex, we would shower and he would lather my body and wash my hair. Kidding around, I would always say one day he was going to break me in half because he was so forceful.

Vincenzo had been on vacation, so I hadn't seen him for about a month. I had plenty of sex in the meantime, but I was dying for him specifically. When we finally reunited, hormones were raging and primal instincts were high. He was fucking me so hard and I was so wet that he slipped out. Upon reentry the force was so great his rock-hard dick crashed into my tailbone and we heard a loud pop. "Are you okay?" I asked. "No!" he screamed. Sex was over immediately. He stood up and started getting dressed before I even knew what happened. I got a glimpse of his penis as he put his pants on. I saw it was bent in half and no longer resembled a penis. Vincenzo rushed to the emergency room and I paced in my living room consulting WebMD. The guilt I felt was indescribable. We prayed it wasn't broken and thankfully it wasn't. What a welcome back greeting! In the next few weeks he made several trips to specialists. His penis was so swollen and it turned black. It was so disgusting! The doctors commented on how violent the sex must have been to cause that disfigurement and he was embarrassed. His recovery was long and I finally saw him again. We had sex once more, very tame sex. After that, I never saw him again, but I bet he will never forget me!

It was very easy to find a new sex partner but impossible to replace my movie buddy. To this day, he is still the only guy I met—vanilla or Lifestyle—who had the exact same taste in films.

Chapter 12. Socks and Soup

Rafael (Challenging FWB, More Friend Than Benefit)

Rafael was a gorgeous Puerto Rican man in his late 40s who looked much younger. He was never married but had two sons from a previous relationship. His body was chiseled like the statue of David due to his cross-fit obsession and strict all-natural diet. He always wore a bandana and had a giant Puerto Rican flag tattoo on his chest, and the names and birthdays of his sons below it. Occasionally, he would smoke pot, give into temptation and binge on greasy, fried food, then hate himself the next morning. Rafael had a fear of commitment and wanted things on his terms. We were like oil and water. He crowed about girls he fucked but got annoyed when I mentioned other guys. He was a total drama queen and we joked he was the girl in our relationship. Rafael was the only single guy I ever met who shared my inner turmoil about the Lifestyle. He was equally plagued by the emotional battle of having fun versus feeling used. We usually hung out at his place and he always ordered me to keep my voice down because he thought I talked too loudly. He was caring and always asked about my family. Some nights we just cuddled on the couch and watched TV. Other nights we got into mischief.

Once I was in the ER and Rafael generously drove my visiting mother to the hospital. It was the only time she inadvertently met a guy I was fucking. Full of questions as usual, she asked how I knew him, what his story was, and so on. Then she commented on how attractive and polite he was and wanted to know why I didn't date him. I laughed to myself—if she only knew! Every once in a while, she still asks about him.

I was in a hotel with a guy going down on me unsuccessfully, killing time because he couldn't get hard, I presumed. I was yawning, wondering how long this would continue before he admitted defeat when my phone vibrated. It is a text from Rafael asking what I was doing. "Not much, you?" I replied. "I'm having some people over—stop by." "Give me 30 min," I texted back. I reached between my legs and tapped the guy on the head. "I'm sorry, there is an emergency—I need to leave." I shot over to Rafael's house, so thankful for my escape. I rang the bell and Rafael answered the door buck naked with a raging hard on. He pulled me inside and kissed me as he slammed the door. Within seconds he tore my clothes off and I was on the couch with his guests, who were also naked and who I had ever met before. The other guy was having performance issues, so Rafael rotated fucking me and the other girl. She was cute, but her voice was irritating, and she wouldn't stop repeating, "Oh my God, this is so hot" as she fondled with my tits, but my night was redeemed.

Another night Rafael called and requested my presence because a girl in his building he was fucking wanted to watch him fuck someone else. I had nothing better to do so I went and fucked him on the couch for her amusement. She and I kissed a little as she touched my body.

Spontaneous adventures were successful, but we failed epically when we tried to plan. A couple reached out to me. They lived an hour away, but she worked in my neighborhood, so we met for happy hour, just us gals. She was in her 40s and resembled Courtney Cox. Her boyfriend was in his 20s and she was trying to break him into the Lifestyle. We chatted about girl stuff and hit it off. She mentioned a single guy she had been planning to meet from my area and I immediately asked if it was Rafael. She said, "Yes." I said, "He is a dear friend." I texted him and invited him to join us for a drink. Maybe planning would turn out better. We got acquainted and decided to have a get-together with the four of us but we never heard from her again. A few weeks later the couple magically resurfaced and Rafael hosted us.

When they arrived, she introduced her boyfriend, who looked nothing like his pictures and was sporting baggy sweatpants and a wrinkled t-shirt. Not a good first impression. He reminded me of an Eminem wannabe. I looked at Rafael and rolled my eyes which meant I was not fucking this kid. We had nowhere else to be, so we hung out for a while to be hospitable. The guys were making drinks in the kitchen while she and I were talking on the couch. She apologized for disappearing, explaining that someone stole her purse which had her prescription pills in it and she was feeling out of it until she could get more. TMI. She was slurring a little. The guys joined us and we shared stories and such. Rafael and I were sitting together on the couch, Eminem was standing before us acting out a scene, and Courtney Cox was curled up on the other couch facing the wall, adding commentary occasionally without

Chapter 12. Socks and Soup

ever looking up. We were watching a train wreck and couldn't look away. This kid was not cut out to be a swinger.

Rafael went to the bathroom and Courtney Cox jumped up, mounted and started kissing me. Didn't see that coming! Her phone started ringing but she ignored it. Ring, ring, ring. Her boyfriend tapped her on the shoulder and said, "Answer your phone, it may be important" as she swatted him away. Ring, ring. Eminem begged her to check. She stood abruptly, thoroughly annoyed, looked at her phone and said, "Why the hell are you calling me while we are in the same room?" What? She was not taking the hint. He wanted the show to stop and they started to argue—he claimed she promised we were just meeting with no intention of playing; he was not prepared for this. Awkward! I snuck off and knocked on the bathroom door, begging Rafael to let me in. I was cracking up as I filled him in on the drama. A few minutes later the shouting voices died down and we went back out, but no one was there. They left? We stood in an empty room confused but thankful. Suddenly the door flew open and Eminem reached for a lighter he left on the counter, and then in a flash he was gone again. We erupted in laughter. Whatever … then we had sex. After that, Rafael and I lost touch. Our lives were going in different directions; it was nothing personal.

About a year later, one Wednesday evening, my phone rang and I was shocked to see the caller ID display Rafael's name. I hadn't seen him in forever. "What are you up to?" he asked. "Absolutely nothing." "I'm going to grab dinner downtown and thought you might care to join me." What a lovely surprise. "Give me thirty minutes to get ready." I quickly freshened up and met him at a local seafood restaurant.

Rafael greeted me with a giant hug. He looked just as handsome as ever, his hair slightly blonder from the summer sun. We ordered a bottle of wine and grilled halibut. Initial conversations covered work, our summers, vacations, and so on. Somehow, we got on the topic of family, specifically our divorced parents and how their splits affected us. We engaged in a very emotional discussion about how we were damaged and that sabotaged our relationships which ended with watery eyes. What the hell was going on? We never had deep talks like this.

All the drama and nonsense we had been involved in faded away and we were just two close friends reconnecting. We barely even mentioned swinging during the two hours we spent together. This was one of my favorite experiences with him. It was more meaningful than any of the freaky sex and orgies we shared. Knowing our friendship was more important than the Lifestyle was refreshing.

The check came, and I offered my credit card, but he insisted on paying. He was so sweet. He walked me to my car and we agreed to keep in touch and hang out more often—whether we had sex or not. The hug goodbye was long, and we parted with a kiss on the cheek. I haven't heard from him since.

Billy (FWB with Intimacy)

I met one of my favorite guys, Billy, from the first Naughty Date I ever posted. I had plans with someone, but he canceled at the last minute. I was pissed. Planning your night around sex only for it not to happen isn't easy. Talk about disappointment! I figured what the hell, I'll try posting an ad and cross my fingers. I was looking for single males only and within an hour I had more than 40 responses, but none met my standards. Now I was really disgruntled. I gave up, threw on my PJs, put on the TV and ate chips.

An hour later I was bored again so I decided to check once more and there he was. This incredibly cute guy wanted to meet me. It was a surprise—like finding a $20 bill in your coat pocket. He wrote, "What I lack in looks I make up for in personality." Oh please! We traded a few emails and then I asked him to call me. The conversation was so easy. We chatted for a half hour about nonsense when I suddenly interrupted. "Not to be rude but do you wanna talk on the phone all night or do this in person?" Billy said, "I'm jumping in the shower, see you in an hour." I texted him an address of a local bar. When he walked in he was exactly my type, maybe the most ideal visually that I ever met.

Billy was an Italian-German-Irish corporate lawyer. Never married, 5'10" with dark hair and a swimmer's shoulders, wearing a gold Rolex his father had given him. Billy was full of the craziest stories and highly entertaining. Normally I stuck to a two-drink max to keep my senses sharp, but Billy and I chugged beers and slammed shots. Time passed as we drank and laughed and talked about anything and everything. He constantly stared at my boobs and was like a loveable teddy bear. The

Chapter 12. Socks and Soup

lights went on and the bar closed. Holy shit, how long did we just hang out without even noticing? Apparently four hours! We moved the party to my house and the sex was dynamite.

We were a sweaty, filthy mess. It was 2 a.m. and my walls were awfully thin, so we woke up the neighbors. They banged on the ceiling. We froze and looked at each other. No way were we ready to stop. "Quick! Mattress on the floor!" I said. Brilliant. He enjoyed slapping me in the face and choking me and got turned on by eye contact. We fucked some more before he left.

We became regular playmates, usually getting together once or twice a month. I received a letter from my neighbors complaining about my incredibly loud sex life. After that, we always went to his house. Our routine was hot, steamy sex followed by cuddling in bed with his Golden Retriever puppy (whom he loved like a baby) while we watched old episodes of *Seinfeld* on Netflix. I found his company soothing and spending a few hours with him was like hitting an internal reset button. I immediately felt refreshed and balanced. He constantly drank Diet Coke and chewed Winterfresh gum. He used the phrase "What's shakin'?" and called me "Pussycat" or "Bella." He always opened doors for me. He was a terrible texter and preferred speaking on the phone.

Billy was the first guy to introduce me to the nude beach scene. It was a Monday, which was referred to as "Strippers and Clippers" because strippers and hairdressers generally had that day off. You could identify the strippers because they left their thongs on to get sexy tan lines. The nude beach was a popular hangout for swingers although you do not need to be a swinger to go. I highly recommend experiencing it with your partner if you are looking for something a little different. It can be empowering for you and sexy for both of you.

The trek from the parking lot to the beach was so long I felt like Moses traveling through the desert. We passed a large volleyball net occupied by four nude male players. The horizon was lined with miniature beach umbrellas that gradually appeared larger as we journeyed closer. The beach was extremely crowded. Billy and I found a vacant spot and spread our blanket on the sand. I sat down and observed my surroundings.

Most of the patrons were serious beachgoers with elaborate setups and fences marking their designated areas. A lot of them had carts with wheels to transport their massive coolers and small tables. They used shovels and mallets helped to secure umbrellas in the sand so they wouldn't blow away in a strong gust of wind. I guess you had to make sure you brought everything you needed because walking back to the car for forgotten items was not happening! It reminded me more of a campsite than a beach and looked like they planned on spending the entire day there. It was a very social scene, large groups of friends chatting and mingling. A typical party—but with no clothes.

Nude bodies swimming or wading in waist-deep water dotted the ocean. It was as if no one realized he or she or anyone else was naked. It was not a big deal. We undressed. Shedding my clothes was like removing the rules of society. Billy rubbed sunscreen on every inch of my body without having to navigate around straps and strings. Holding hands, we strolled down to the shore. I am a water lover, and let me tell you, there is nothing as incredible as being naked in the ocean. It was so freeing! A total paradise.

I glanced around and was impressed that most people on the beach were not in excellent shape. I noted a lot of large bellies, sagging tits, and hairy bushes. A surprisingly number of ass cheek tattoos and genital piercings. Everyone was welcome here and you didn't need to be a supermodel to proudly flaunt your body. No judgment. Beachgoers ranged from senior citizens to young couples to families with infants. A few people remained clothed and I wondered why they were there. Why come to a nude beach and not embrace it? After the initial shock wore off we enjoyed just another day at the beach. I forgot we were naked.

I sporadically felt a few pairs of eyes gawking at me, mostly from single guys. Otherwise, when someone said hello, he or she looked at my eyes, not my exposed body. Being there was natural.

Many might assume a nude beach is filled with a bunch of horny people engaging in naughty behavior, but in fact such behavior is strictly prohibited. Closed tents are not permitted, and security officers patrol the area to ensure no inappropriate touching occurs.

Feeling the salt water against my flesh with no fabric as a barrier, letting my tits bounce in the waves with no supportive underwire was glorious. Billy and I hugged and kissed, and he held me in his arms as I floated completely carefree. There was something personal sharing this experience with him. We didn't know anyone else at the beach, so we remained in our own little bubble. The background disappeared and all I focused on was him, us.

Our relationship was intimate and after a year I asked if he wanted to date. Deep down I'm sure I knew we were not a good romantic match, but I was in one of those moods where I rolled the dice. Closing my eyes and throwing a dart at a board. Either I got a bulls-eye and he said yes or I missed the target and he said no. Billy declined, claiming he was not over his ex and not emotionally available. Unlike Peter, he was genuinely tortured over the decision and told me I deserved someone who could treat me right. He encouraged me to find someone better than him. I appreciated that. We stopped speaking for two months to cool down then thankfully reconnected.

Ricky (Somewhere Between NSA and FWB)

Ricky was few years younger than me, mid-20s and super cocky. Greek with dark features, he was a private gym owner who fancied fast motorcycles and older women. He wasn't my type, but he was persistent. We chatted online for a while and he begged for the chance to talk on the phone. I clearly remember being an asshole and saying, "You have to guess my phone number." I gave him six of the digits. How obnoxious was I? If he really wanted me he would figure it out. A little later my phone rang. We talked for a decent amount of time and there was definite chemistry. We had an interesting flirtatious connection and his infectious personality grew on me.

He convinced me to meet him for a drink. I was dressed very casually, not expecting this to go anywhere, but Ricky's confidence and devilish smile drew me in. We wanted to have sex, but we had nowhere to go. I didn't even have my car—it was in the shop following a fender-bender and I had to take an Uber. Ricky said, "Let's go to my training studio and play and then I'll drive you home." I said, "Are you fucking nuts? I'm not crossing multiple county lines with a stranger, fucking you in a gym and then hoping you really drive me all the way back home. No way!" But I simply could not resist his charm so ten minutes later we were in his car speeding down the highway. I prayed I wouldn't end up a missing person on an episode of *Dateline*.

We went to his studio and had insanely good sex on a pile of towels we spread on the hardwood floor. So classy! His cock was long, and he reached spots inside me so deep I swore he was going to rupture an organ. He loved when I licked his balls and told him how much I craved his big dick. And yes, he did in fact drive me home after—*whew*!

Ricky and I became somewhat close and usually saw each other at random hours, very late at night. He spoke three languages, had an affinity for wacky socks and never wore underwear. We discussed our escapades and laughed a lot since we shared a sarcastic sense of humor. We normally fucked other people right before or right after we saw each other. We were both high in demand. We didn't care. We were amused by it.

There was this gorgeous guy who lived two hours away. We desperately wanted to meet but I worked days and he worked nights. In the meantime, we got carried away and texted 24/7—personal stuff, sex stuff, everything. When the opportunity arose, we met at the swinger-friendly bar. I was bummed because Max, who frequented the joint, was not going to be there.

I knocked on the hotel room door and was dressed in a black trench coat and lingerie (yes, people really do that!) the first time I laid eyes on him. European, six feet tall, bald, muscular. I entered the room and we couldn't get down to business fast enough. After about five minutes, he came. Hmm. Not what I expected. "I'm sorry," he said. "I have been so excited to meet you, but give me a minute and I'll be ready for more." Fair enough, I figured, we have all night. But this occurred three or four more times in a row. He could not control himself and after a while it got awkward. All those fantasies and expectations not being met. Guys get very uncomfortable about their performance issues. Damage control time. I said, "Let's go to the bar and grab a drink, loosen up." As we walked through the bar I was distracted and totally bumped right into someone—Ricky!

We were both startled and shared a big hug. I respectfully introduced Ricky to my date, who was not amused. He started questioning us about our relationship and we were honest—we were swingers, after all. His body language changed, and he wanted to protect his territory. He stood by my side and became oddly serious. Ricky and I secretly whispered, "Too bad this guy is so uptight—we could've just had a threesome." The three of us had a drink and then Ricky left to meet a housewife he regularly fucked. My date was pretty much ruined as the guy could not cope with the fact I fucked other guys. Are you kidding me? We spent a very awkward night in the hotel. The next morning, he woke up super early and snuck out. I texted Ricky who lived nearby and invited him to the hotel. He fucked me for a few hours on the other guy's dime. Perfectly ironic. The moral of the story is you don't invest too much of yourself before meeting because nothing matters until you are face to face. Feeling like you know someone does not mean you do.

Chapter 13

Triangular Fun

A large percentage of couples were over 40. Their reasons for swinging ranged from they already had kids and now had time for themselves; they needed an extra spark after years of marriage; they had different sexual needs; they simply loved sex; or, like my ex and me, they were looking to add another dimension of excitement to an already wondrous sex life. One partner may have openly admitted he or she could not be monogamous, so swinging was an alternative to cheating.

Personally, I preferred older couples. Couples swinging in their 20s and couples seeking their first experience make me uneasy. They may have excellent sexual skills, but I remembered my mentality in those circumstances. I was insecure and not completely trusting. They probably hadn't been in the Lifestyle long enough to have worked out all the kinks.

Most couples are married, but some are just dating, or two singles can partner to act as a couple. The joke is that a lot of couples are hot wives and not-so-hot husbands. It can be extremely hard to find a couple in which both people are equally attractive. Couples can be both straight, both bi, or, most commonly, straight male and bi female. Some are soft swap, full swap, same room but different beds, different rooms, and some have "hall passes" to play individually. Some want other couples, some want straight single guys for MFM threesomes, bi single guys for MMF threesomes, and just about all of them want a girl for the magical and coveted FMF threesome. Others are "hot wives" or seeking "bulls" for "cuckold" meaning the husband just watches other guys with his wife. He may or may not participate. He may send her to the guy alone and ask for pictures and videos of them together. Other couples are into

Chapter 13. Triangular Fun

gang bangs where the wife fucks several guys at once. Again, the possibilities are endless. A lot of couples have a no kissing policy which I understood in the beginning but now I always find laughable. That is their "sacred, private thing." Sure, kissing is more personal than having his penis inside me or your pussy in his mouth? OK. Keep telling yourself that. To me that is a red flag for jealousy and insecurity. They try to maintain some control by keeping something just for themselves.

There are also couples in which the girl is clearly swinging just to please her man. You can tell because he is forceful and she is reluctant. Some couples will only play with married couples, meaning they refrain from two singles acting as a couple because a non-committed couple may threaten their relationship.

Arranging dates with couples could be precarious because we must juggle three schedules plus the couple may need to hire a babysitter. Also, since there were two women we had to plan around two menstrual cycles. That could automatically cancel two weeks out of the month. Factor in distance and coordinating could take months.

When conversing with couples it was usually preferred for me to have contact with the female. All correspondence went through her to avoid any suspicious behavior. In cases where the husband oversaw communications, I asked to have the wife attached to a group text, so she had full knowledge of what transpired. I never wanted to be involved in an inappropriate exchange behind the wife's back. It was impossible to know how much the husband would tell her versus what he would hide. I could never be too careful when a marriage was on the line.

For the first few months on the site I only met single guys. It was nerve wracking enough meeting one stranger, let alone two! But after a while, as anything else you do, you get more brazen and want to attempt another level.

Couples offered a remarkable dynamic because I was briefly being invited into their world, their relationship. Would I have better chemistry with one half of the couple or would the three of us have equal passion? I could enjoy the soft skin of the woman and the hard cock of the guy. Having four hands and two mouths to please me added extra sensations. Now, if one was eating my pussy, the other could kiss me. He could be fucking me from behind while she sucked on my tits. I was thoroughly engrossed observing how they behaved toward each other in my presence. Did me being there bring them closer or put a wedge between them?

Couples were an indulgence, a hot fudge sundae, if you will—fun to splurge occasionally but not part of my daily diet. They produced a short-lived sugar rush but provided no substantial protein. I could not survive on them alone.

Couples: Jack and Linda

Jack and Linda were in their late 40s, attractive, friendly, very secure. Jack was straight, on the shorter side but in good shape, with a military buzz cut and glasses. He was a firefighter. Linda was an extremely busty bisexual redhead with kind hazel eyes. She was a high school English teacher. We met for drinks and I confessed I was new at this. They assured me I was in safe hands. They were so down to earth, and we laughed a lot as we nibbled on appetizers. There was chemistry, so we decided to go to the nearby hotel where Jack had made a reservation, just in case. I was internally freaking out—this was real now. Somehow the hotel was overbooked, and Jack could not actually get the room, so we agreed to continue another time. Both kissed me goodnight in the parking lot. I was half relieved and half terrified knowing I had to do this all over again. I was much better being spontaneous than scheduled in these situations. Overthinking can be your enemy.

A few weeks later I went to their house. I'll never forget, it was 9 on a Thursday morning—very random but the only time we were all free. We chatted in the kitchen and I drank water because I hate coffee. They explained they had recently renovated the house and did all the work themselves, pointing out the tile floors, large bay window and wood beams across the ceiling. I could barely focus on the conversation because the anticipation of the unknown was so strong. Finally, they offered me a tour of the house and my stomach dropped. Showtime. Living room, office, spare bedroom ... master bedroom. Deep breath. I wandered into the master bathroom and the fact that it was painted red somehow comforted me. If she liked red, she must be cool. Logical assumption, right? Ha!

There was a king-size bed opposite a large window overlooking the driveway. Linda said, "I'll be right back." I stood at the edge of the bed and tensed as Jack grabbed my face and kissed me. I froze. I kept thinking Linda was going to tromp in and smack me for stealing her man, but nothing happened. I cautiously kissed him back. I felt her approach from behind and then she kissed me too. Whew! In that moment I knew I would be okay. The three of us had a blast—my first successful threesome! Classical music played softly in the background as Jack took turns fucking us. Linda went down on me as I sucked his cock. She kissed me and twisted my nipples while I rode him. It felt natural and comfortable. They later confessed they were technically in their early 50s. They found that when they listed their true ages, they were only contacted by older people. Lowering their ages increased their visibility during searches on the site. It was totally understandable. Age really is just a number. They currently hold the title of oldest people I fucked.

As I was leaving I joked, "Wow, I feel like I survived a deadly roller coaster and should get a souvenir." The next time I saw them they gave me a magnet Linda made which read "I survived my first threesome." I adored it. It was red. I still have it hanging on my fridge—but I take it down when vanilla people come over or it would lead to a lot of questions! I saw them a few more times. Linda even invited me to a casino to surprise Jack for his birthday. It was not the first time I was a birthday present for someone's husband. Jack and Linda proved that there are normal couples out there just looking to have some fun.

Mitch and Carla

I came across a couple looking for their first FMF. We had a mutual connection, Jack and Linda. We met for sushi and talked over a few glasses of wine. They were lovely people. Mitch, an accountant, was white, in his mid–40s, decent looking, not as fit as I preferred, but polite and funny. Carla, a stay-at-home mom, was Asian with dark flowing hair, wide brown eyes and the longest eyelashes I had ever seen. After dinner, we went to the hotel room where dozens of candles surrounded a massage table. Giving a pretty girl a sexy massage as foreplay was part of Carla's ultimate fantasy. Score! I was so flattered! She rubbed oil all over me as she caressed my body with Mitch admiring from a distance.

After the massage Carla and I moved to the bed where we made out and she went down on me. Mitch and I kissed, and I briefly sucked his cock, but we had little interaction because this was more about Carla's desires than his. It was a very passionate, sensual experience. It demonstrated that couples were living out real fantasies and I was a part of the experience. I felt I served a purpose and their gratitude was so sincere. It was a noticeable shift from the meaningless hardcore fuck sessions I was accustomed to.

The following week I unexpectedly ran into Mitch and Carla at a party I attended with Peter (obviously, this was before our demise). They were with another couple I didn't know, or did I? They looked so familiar, or at least he did. I was sure I knew him, so I kept searching my brain for the context. I suddenly turned to him and blurted out, "I have been in your bed." I am so goofy sometimes. What a thing to say—even among swingers. He looked at me confused and his lady rightfully shot me a dirty look. I was embarrassed and scrambled to explain my way out of this mess. I said, "I was definitely in your house a long time ago with my ex-boyfriend Elliot." I told him my name and his eyes lit up as he remembered. He refreshed his partner's memory by whispering something in her ear. Once she made the connection we all freaked out and hugged. Elliot and I had met Brian and Sandy online about six years before and played at their house. The experience was a little blurry because it was so long ago, but we agreed we all had fun. Sandy had changed her hair—that was why I didn't recognize her right away—but we had a graphic girl-girl session which included her fist in my vagina and that was impossible to forget. I never got the chance to fuck Brian because Elliot and I were not full swap then. Luckily, I was a free agent these days and had no rules!

The scene was dying down so Mitch and Carla invited me, Peter, Brian and Sandy back to their hotel room for a private party. There were two beds and it was customary to play on one and leave the other untouched, so the hosts could sleep in a clean bed. The six of us piled onto the designated bed and it became a game of naked Twister—body parts tangled and contorted. I didn't know who was touching me or whose genitals were in my face, but it didn't matter—we were all friends. Once the soft swap simmered down each guy fucked his woman.

On the drive home Peter and I both wondered why no one fucked anyone else. He regretted not fucking Carla and I was surprised Brian did not try to fuck me. The next morning Sandy and I texted, and I casually mentioned our curiosity. We realized the men were so respectful that they were all waiting for someone else to make the first move. No one wanted to appear too forceful since we all failed to verbalize our boundaries beforehand. I asked Sandy if she and Brian would care to see me and Peter. A few weeks later Peter and I drove to their house (to pick up where Elliot and I had left off years ago). This was our first attempt at full swapping together and anticipation was high.

Brian and Sandy

During the drive Peter and I speculated about how the night would unfold.

Brian was tall with wavy shoulder-length hair and tattoos covering both arms and his back. He cherished Scotch, jazz music, his leather jacket and his convertible. Sandy was petite with a small chest, auburn hair in a pixie cut, and a diamond tongue stud. She was cute but not hot, but her personality made up for it. Sandy and I gossiped in the corner while Peter and Brian bonded over a beer. Uninterested in their discussion about sports, Sandy and I plotted to go upstairs to the spare room and get the party started. I laid down on the bed and she crawled on top of me and we made out a bit before she went down on me. She was using the vibrator on me when the two guys appeared in the doorway. "It's about time," I taunted them. They joined us on the pull-out sofa bed, but it was too crowded, so Peter and Sandy opted for the floor while Brian and I remained on the bed. Brian loved eating my pussy and did so for a long time before he fucked me missionary style. We switched, and I got on top. I rode him so hard the bed collapsed. We laughed hysterically for a second then continued fucking on the crooked bed. Nothing we couldn't work around.

Sandy and Brian and I became instant friends. I went to their house and we had super-hot threesomes. We even spent a New Year's Eve together. I was their Unicorn for a long time, but I eventually lost touch with them. They were not married, and their relationship was very rocky—always on and off. I think she grew envious about the chemistry Brian and I had.

I hadn't spoken to them for a long time when I noticed a new profile for a single guy and immediately recognized his faceless photos. I emailed him to say hi and asked what was up. Brian informed me he and Sandy had officially broken up six months ago and he was ready to date again. My profile stated I was seeking a possible long-term relationship and Brian admitted he always had strong feelings for me and hoped we could reconnect. A few minutes later he called and invited me to a BBQ at his house that same afternoon. I was reluctant because it was an hour drive and I was feeling lazy but ultimately agreed to go. The weather was beautiful, so I might as well enjoy it. We hung out with his vanilla friends and he was attentive and affectionate.

That night we had sex alone for the first time and it was almost awkward, unnatural. The bed felt too large and empty. Having him to myself was bizarre because we always had threesomes or other couples involved—at least Sandy. Having each other's full attention now made the sex more intimate and the focus more intense. I saw him twice more, but he displayed signs of a controlling nature, so I ended our relationship.

The experience with Brian and Sandy taught me that some couples are not strong enough to participate in the Lifestyle. Jealousy could pose a real threat even if it wasn't my intention and I was not a permanent fixture.

Mark and Gina

With four kids and two jobs, Mark and Gina had crazy schedules. Not to mention they lived two and a half hours away. Whenever we made plans they cancelled at the last minute. After a while I gave up and accepted we would never meet. Sometimes it was just not meant to be. Contact became limited to an occasional text from Mark saying "Hi" or "Thinking of you." Then one day I was at work and out of the blue he texted me announcing they were coming to my area in a few days and wanted to meet. Finally! I couldn't pass up this remarkable invitation, so I bailed on my plans with my vanilla friends. I thought my decision was justified.

I met Mark and Gina for drinks in the lobby of an upscale hotel. Mark was average height and build, white, cute and witty. Gina was bubbly, had dark hair and a body like mine and she wore a short black leather skirt that flared out slightly. There was a very natural vibe, so we went upstairs to have some adult fun. Gina was extremely bi, so we engaged in girl-girl and swapped fucking Mark. When she asked if we could try her new strap on, I said, "I'm feeling adventurous, so sure, what the hell." New experiences were always welcomed. I positioned myself on all fours and arched my ass so she could have easier entry to my pussy. The foreign object pushed deep inside me and within a few minutes the sensation shifted from pleasure to severe pain. I asked her to stop and ran to the bathroom. My crotch was bright red, swollen and burning. I wanted to cry. My Sherlock skills of deduction led me conclude the dildo had latex in it which I was highly allergic to! The most unsexy moment ever! Thankfully we were all cool and handled the situation swiftly. Mark ran down the hall to get me ice while Gina apologized profusely. It wasn't her fault, though, just a freak accident. We hung out and talked while I iced my vagina and then we went to a bar and had more drinks. We partied until 5 in the morning when I had to go straight to work. I left my favorite belt in the hotel, so they kindly mailed it to me. We keep in touch but have been unable to hang out again.

That night I learned you need to have a good sense of humor and not be easily embarrassed. Be able to go with the flow because plans could go awry in the blink of an eye!

M&M

Meghan and Mike were one of my favorite couple experiences. Most couples I met were over 40 Meghan and Mike were my age, early 30s. As usual they emailed me looking for a FMF threesome. Mike was exactly my type, athletic body, slicked back dark hair, a few tattoos on his arms. In one picture, he stood very erect, wearing only a pair of tight white boxer briefs with his arms behind his back and a look in his eyes that screamed confidence. Meghan was petite with big blue eyes and long, bouncy blonde curls. Photos showed her tiny perky breasts with pink nipples and a belly button ring. Maybe she was a cheerleader in high school. She reminded me of a girl you could see in a commercial for one of those cheesy 800 hotlines. Poses of her looking over her shoulder or biting her lower lip and staring away from the camera portrayed her as the innocent girl who wants to be naughty. I'm sure most guys would die to fuck her. I found her pretty, but blondes weren't my thing.

After a few emails Meghan requested a phone call to voice verify (prove I was a girl). Normally I didn't do that, but I agreed. I mean, I had nothing to hide. To our surprise, our quick call turned into an hour-long conversation. They had never actually met a single girl from the site before and Meghan was fascinated. She was insanely curious about my experiences and wanted to know how I got into the Lifestyle. Did I enjoy it? She was sympathetic to the dangers and hardships I must face as a single girl and said she admired me for being so tough. She didn't think she would survive in my shoes. She was amiable, so sincere and concerned.

Ironically, they lived a few blocks away from Peter, so we met at the same bar where I had first met him. As we sat at the bar drinking our beers I occasionally glanced over my shoulder toward the front door. I would've loved to see the look on his face if he happened to stroll into his favorite local hangout and find me with these two hotties. (Peter had previously expressed interest in meeting them but knew they didn't allow single guys. He had casually asked if I wanted to bring him along for a foursome sometime. I declined. I wasn't about to be his meal ticket.)

Meghan and Mike were both chatty and outgoing. After the second drink Mike suggested we relocate to their nearby apartment. They lived on the ground level of a modern building with a mirrored wall along the lobby and sleek, gray leather couches flanked by large vases overflowing with giant green leaves. I removed my shoes in their foyer and draped my jacket over the back of a clear acrylic chair tucked under the round white dining table. A small crystal chandelier dimly lit the room. Meghan escorted me to the white leather L-shaped couch while Mike offered me a drink from the kitchen. "Red wine, please," I replied.

Boxes were piled in the corner and they told me their wedding date was approaching and they were in the process of buying a house. I congratulated them. With formalities out of the way, Mike suggested we continue in the bedroom. A king-sized bed commandeered most of the space in it. The platform was so high I had a hard time climbing aboard. White satin sheets and two gold sconces glowing with red lightbulbs gave the bedroom a brothel-type atmosphere.

Meghan kissed me first. She turned to Mike and said, "You need to try this." It was like offering your friend a bite of your delicious dessert at a restaurant. Mike quickly accepted the invitation. He was so fucking sexy. As we kissed she methodically removed my jeans and panties. Her cool fingers slid inside me and I moaned. He removed my shirt and kissed my chest. She unhooked my bra. I noticed how coordinated these two were. They worked as a well choreographed team to seduce me.

Meghan asked to watch Mike fuck me. He put a condom on and drove his hard cock deep inside me. He felt amazing. Meghan knelt beside me petting my hair and shouting instructions at Mike like a football coach training an athlete. "Fuck her harder, baby." "Make her scream." "Flip her over." He obeyed and repositioned me on all fours. The fucking reconvened and Meghan urged him to slap my ass. I was caught off guard when, without warning, she grabbed a fistful of my hair and called me a dirty little slut as she reached her other hand beneath me to rub my clit. Holy shit—these two were fucking wild! What a treat.

Next, she directed me to get on top and ride her man. I obliged as any well-behaved houseguest would. With my arms braced against the headboard I fucked him so hard he was speechless. Meghan was in heaven. She randomly interjected by pulling my hair or choking me. The combination of desire and naughtiness was overwhelmingly erotic. Sweat dripped down my back and my cheeks were quite flushed so, reluctantly, we had to take a water break before I passed out. Round two was equally lengthy and pleasurable. I had several more vigorous orgasms and Mike eventually came all over my back and let out a hefty cry of relief.

I was a guest at their house twice more. Then they got married and their attention shifted to the honeymoon and redecorating. They sadly but understandably disappeared. From them I witnessed two people seriously on the same page, working in unison to strengthen their bond. Swinging added to their relationship and their love.

Douchebags (Third Scary Night)

A couple that played exclusively with single girls emailed me. Max knew other single girls who had met the pair previously and he had heard positive things about them. I'm not sure why I wasn't that interested—something about their pictures. They were attractive but seemed too perfect, staged or almost fake. It was hard to pinpoint but my gut had a negative reaction. We communicated back and forth and they kept inviting me to their house. I told them I didn't travel, and I didn't go to houses. They were bizarrely persistent which annoyed me, and looking back, I should have stopped it right there. A few days later there was a meet and greet nearby, and somehow I agreed to meet them there. It turned out we had several mutual acquaintances which made me a little less cynical.

She was petite, possibly a size zero with huge fake tits, manicured nails, and her features reminded me of the singer Shania Twain. He was around six feet tall, had a tan complexion and a bald head, and was exotic looking, maybe Persian. The party was lame, but I was just in one of those troublemaker moods—bad combination—so I was persuaded to go their house which was not too far away. It was a mansion, huge but sparsely furnished. I thought that was odd. It had a sterile feel to it. Not cozy and inviting.

As soon as we got upstairs, I grew uneasy. Not sure why, just instinct. I sat on the bed and the wife started blowing him in front of the armoire. She didn't seem into it, and there was no moaning from either of them. Silence filled the room and you could have heard a pin drop which made their actions feel cold, mechanical and routine. I sat in my underwear wondering how I could get out of there. I was daydreaming about what clever excuse I could use when she suddenly ran out of the bedroom and into the bathroom. A moment later, sounds of vomiting echoed through the halls. YES!!! A devilish smile crept onto my face. I was free! I stood up to get dressed and the husband approached me. "Where do you think you are going? We are just getting started." "You need to take care of your wife, let's do this another time," I said politely as I collected my clothes. He kissed me, and I pulled away. He grabbed my arm and pushed me onto the bed. More vomiting in the distance. I jumped up, defiant. With my heart racing I stared him dead in the eye, and with a look that told him I was not fucking around, said, "I am leaving." He threw his hands up and backed away. I stormed out and texted Max to vent my outrage.

The next day she texted me to apologize and offered to send him to me. I declined. She practically begged me to fuck him and her insistence enraged me. No is supposed to mean no. I finally lost my temper and sent a lengthy message proclaiming I was not their toy, they needed to learn some manners, and I would never fuck him in a million years. They still reach out periodically, but I just ignore them.

This episode instilled the importance of listening to my gut, never forgetting that some people were only concerned with what they wanted and if I wasn't careful I could be left feeling violated. This was a classic case of being objectified.

Kelly and Jorge

I had been in such a great mood that I craved something out of the ordinary. I hadn't attempted a couple in ages, so I scrolled through my many unopened emails. On the fifth page, I found what I was searching for. Kelly and Jorge played with couples occasionally but preferred single girls since Kelly was extremely bi and absolutely loved watching Jorge fuck other women. Kelly could've been Kate Hudson's twin sister with her long, straight bleach-blonde hair and precisely cut bangs. At 49 Jorge had the body of a man ten years younger. He was nicely toned and tan with grey scattered through his jet-black hair. Kelly and I texted briefly, and I informed her I would be out of town for the next week and would contact her when I returned.

As promised, I reached out to them to set up a date and the following Saturday they drove up to visit me. It was a warm summer night and the downtown area was bustling. The outdoor seating in front of the restaurants was packed and felt too crowded to have intimate conversations, so I suggested a bar inside one of the less popular places.

I walked in and spotted Kelly and Jorge at the bar, gave a quick double hug hello, one with each arm, and said, "I'll be right back" as I raced to the bathroom. I had been guzzling water all day due to the heat and it was catching up with me. I was pleased with their appearances, I thought as I peed. I walked back to the bar at a normal, relaxed pace.

Kelly drank vodka and tonic while Jorge drank a Heineken and I ordered a Yuengling. Kelly sat on a stool, Jorge and I stood. The energy was warm and friendly, and I had a good feeling about the night ahead. We chatted about our jobs and the relentless heat, our shoes and the neighborhood. After the first round, we moved to a booth to order food. Kelly and I sat on the curved white leather couch while Jorge sat in a chair opposite us. After ordering a salad to share, appetizers and a second round of beverages, we got down to business. It was like a button was pressed and we efficiently moved from casual banter to talk about sex. They were both divorced and had been dating for three years but living separately. Kelly had been the instigator in their entry into swinging as her strong desire for women led her to invite her girlfriends into their bed.

Kelly was without a doubt the dominant half of the couple, which was unusual. She did most of the talking and her eyes lit up when she told stories of their past threesomes. She was one of the least jealous women I ever met, and imagining me with Jorge practically made her drool. Jorge was quieter and fidgety as he drank his beers quickly but hardly ate. Kelly teased him about being nervous.

Kelly excused herself to the ladies' room and Jorge asked if I wanted to taunt her. "Sure." He slid into her vacant seat in the booth beside me and asked, "Do you mind if I touch you?" "Of course not. That's what we are here for." He put his arm around my shoulder and explained the plan for us to be kissing when she returned. "It would drive her wild." We started kissing and after some effort our tongues became acquainted. It was not a spectacular kiss, but it improved. After a few minutes, I stopped and said, "Does she always take this long?" He laughed. "No, I bet she is waiting to make sure I made a move on you." We continued to kiss, and she finally arrived for the show. As promised, Kelly was ecstatic. She sat down on Jorge's other side, sandwiching him in between two very hot and very horny women.

Chapter 13. Triangular Fun

The hotel was a five-minute drive away, and they offered me a ride even though I had my own car. I felt safe with them, so I accepted. Jorge drove, and Kelly ordered me to sit in the front seat so she could watch us flirt from the back. We checked in and headed for the fourth floor.

We all took turns in the bathroom. Jorge was last on the list, so Kelly and I were alone on the bed. She looked at me and cautiously asked if she could touch me, knowing my profile was still listed as straight. I nodded, said, "Absolutely," and admitted I hadn't touched a woman in a long time. She grabbed my face and kissed me, wet, sloppy, porn-style kisses. Jorge entered the room and leaned against the dresser. Kelly and I continued to kiss, and she wrestled me onto my back. My shirt came up, and her hands explored my tits. As my head rolled to one side I noticed Jorge texting, which I thought was odd. What could be more interesting than us? She unbuttoned my pants and I no longer cared about Jorge. I was too distracted by her long pink manicured nails entering my pussy.

I moaned with delight. She was doing a great job. Surprisingly rough and aggressive like a guy. Jorge announced he had to step out to take a phone call and Kelly was agitated. She pried herself off me and followed him to the door. I could hear angry whispering in the hallway. Kelly returned alone and apologized for his behavior, claiming he was just nervous, and said we could play until he was ready. She resumed the position of her mouth on mine and her fingers inside me. After about five minutes Kelly called for a break and called him from her cell. She spoke firmly as if scolding a child for misbehaving. I was growing slightly concerned. "He will be right up," she promised, and our play continued. If I was getting pleased I didn't care who was touching me. I was enjoying this girl-girl encounter more than I expected.

Still, no Jorge. Kelly called him a final time and was pissed. She ended the call and said she regretted to inform me the night was prematurely over. The expression on her face led me to assume the long car ride home would not be pleasant for him!

We dressed quickly as I tried to calm her. "It happens," I said. "No worries." In the parking lot Jorge was pacing, talking on his phone, his voice raised. Kelly and I climbed into the car and he joined us after he hung up. "Family emergency," he said with a frown as he drove me back to my car. The next day Kelly texted me to remind me she had a great time and hoped to see me again. They never got back in touch.

That night taught me some women were much more aggressive than their guys and sometimes they were the ones being weighed down by their men.

Chapter 14

Extra M's

After one-on-ones with single guys and FMF threesomes with couples, I ventured into two guys for MFM threesomes. And once I did, I discarded my bi-friendly episodes. I was hooked on as much cock as possible. I didn't need another woman in my way.

I had been talking to a guy who was experienced and well credited. Positive we would get along, we skipped a few of the formalities. No drink at a bar. No meeting at a public place. Fuck it. Kevin came directly to my apartment one Friday afternoon, and as per his request, I opened the door wearing a see-through bra and fishnet panties. His eyes were wide. He was not expecting me to really do that, I guess. Immediately I kissed him and led him to my bedroom. I was so ready. We started fooling around and then we kept fooling around … hmm … I thought progress was unexpectedly slow considering all the plans we had for each other. Oh wait—he can't get hard. Good Lord. What's wrong? Why doesn't he like me? Finally Kevin humbly said, "I'm sorry, I don't know what's wrong." I lost interest, so he jerked off sitting next to me. I didn't know what to do so I tried to avoid eye contact. After, he sat on the bed and started babbling to distract from the current situation. I pretended to listen to be polite, but my mind was already wandering to what I would eat for dinner and if the nail salon would be open late enough for me to get a pedicure. If he wasn't going to satisfy me I really had no other use for him. I just wanted him to leave so I could get on with my day. I never spoke to him again.

A few months later I got a random text from him asking what I was doing. Coincidentally, it was my day off, so I responded, "Nothing. Sitting in my apartment bored." Kevin admitted he felt bad for not pleasing me and said I intimidated him because I was so forward. Crappy excuse, I thought as I rolled my eyes. If I had a dollar for every time I heard that, I'd be rich. He offered to make it up to me. "I have a cute friend; we can have a threesome." I said, "Oh?"—just to humor him—"when?" "How about right now, one hour," Kevin replied. I jumped up from my couch and paced. I had always wanted a MFM threesome but I wasn't prepared. Something this major required proper warning and planning. I wasn't even waxed! I was silent for a few minutes. "Are you still there?" he asked. Considering the uniqueness of the opportunity, I blurted, "Fuck it. Sure, why not."

I panicked and called Max to ask for tips. I was talking so fast I was incoherent. "Calm down, you will be fine. You are a fun girl." He suggested positions and made me promise to call him after. I frantically showered, shaved, dressed and headed to the motel in record time. In the car, I gave myself a pep talk. The motel was a short drive away which was good because I didn't have time to convince myself to chicken out.

I parked and asked him for the room number: 97. I walked up to the second level and, with a deep inhale, I knocked on the door. I was perspiring. The door creaked open, and I nonchalantly said, "Hey, what's up?" as if this was a typical occurrence. Kevin introduced me to his friend and I was relieved that he was cute. The room was a little dingy, not at all like the nice hotels I was used to.

I went to the bathroom and put cold water on my face. I removed my pants and top but left my socks on due to the questionable cleanliness of the carpet. To keep the momentum going, I exited the bathroom in a stringy thong and a lacy bra. They both stared at me with open mouths as I climbed onto the bed without saying a word. I figured if I acted confident I could fool them. The action started immediately. Kissing, touching, all three of us intertwined. The mirror on the ceiling added an element of kinkiness. I loved watching our tangled limbs as I was devoured. It amused me when they verbally coordinated positions and cheered each other on as they traded turns. Mostly I sucked a dick or kissed one while the other fucked me. They had a "bromance" vibe about them.

Within an hour, both guys came, and it was over. I was puzzled. "There are two of you! How can you be done when I want more?" They were exhausted and shocked I was still horny. My self-esteem was increasing. "If you ever call me again you should bring a third guy for back-up," I teased.

That rendezvous taught me to trust my inner sex goddess. There was no need to fear the unknown or assume I would be the one doing the disappointing. Knowing I could handle a new situation eased my nerves about it.

It was a great first threesome, but I knew for a fact it was a tame PG-13 (in the swinging world) experience and it made me strive for a wilder, X-rated encounter. After all, what is life without goals?

Chapter 15

Limo Luis

I had a lot of rules and restrictions. They made me feel in control, or so I thought. For example, no anal—non-negotiable. It was painful and way too personal. No black guys (no offense, just my preference). No facials (ejaculating on my face—I mean, gross!). No husbands playing solo (no need for drama). Then I met the man with the plan. Boundaries disappeared, limits vanished and fantasies I didn't even know I had were realized.

I had been complaining to Max that my dream of a salacious MFM threesome had eluded me. Specifically, the goal was DV (double vaginal, yep, two dicks in your vagina at once—it's a real thing). Some people want to go skydiving or go on a safari but fucking two guys simultaneously was my bucket list item. However, with my requirements it was not easy to pull off, even being a Unicorn. Several problems arose. Many guys are jealous. Some are homophobic even though both are straight. If I was half of a couple, it would be easy to find one single guy and make my aspirations come true. But now I needed to find two random guys, whose personalities meshed and who had similar styles of sex, were not competitive and had equal stamina. I had a lot of requirements. Max, God bless him, had the perfect guy. He sent me Luis's profile and I liked what I saw.

They had met at a small hotel party Luis hosted and successfully performed DV on a girl. They were an established team. In a world where profiles are filled with rock-hard abs and dick pics, Luis's profile had him in a clown suit. Literally, a Halloween costume. I swear to God, I couldn't make this up if I tried. Immediately I was fascinated and needed to know this eccentric man. It was a couple's profile and it said they were allowed to play alone. Ugh. I didn't like the sound of that but something about his pictures drew me in. I read their 50-plus credits and popular opinion was this guy was larger than life, one of a kind. I broke my first rule about married guys and told Max I was in.

Luis (FWB to the Extreme, One of My Favorite People in the World)

Luis called and conducted a professional business interview. What did I want to try? What were my expectations? My goals? From 1 to 10, how intense should he be? What were my parameters? How long did I want him there? So many questions I was unprepared for. His voice was so smooth, and he assured me my pleasure was his only concern and I believed him. We set a date for New Year's Eve.

That night I drove to the chosen hotel, trying to imagine how the night would unfold. I was usually calm before meeting guys, but I was so nervous about Luis. DV was a big deal. I arrived first and went to the bar. Max texted me that he was running late which added to my anxiety. Luis appeared and sat next to me. He was large in stature, had dark, brooding eyes, and he wore a baseball cap. I was incredibly intimidated by his energy and presence. We ordered drinks even though neither of us really drank. It just seemed appropriate since we were sitting at a bar. He spoke softly and told me he had been looking forward to meeting me. He had never had another guy bring him a single girl. Luis was used to being the ringleader and organizing gatherings. The change in dynamic was highly enticing to him.

He lightly touched my diamond-studded belt buckle as he complimented it. I felt an electric pulse between us and I got goose bumps. He stared at me like a hungry wolf stares at a wounded deer. There was no doubt I was in for the time of my life—and I thought for a second I was in way over my head. I texted Max: "Where the fuck are you? HURRY UP!" Luis informed me he needed time to prepare the room. I didn't know what that meant, and I was petrified to find out. Luis and I proceeded upstairs to the room where he gave me an outfit to change into. He ordered me to go in the bathroom and not come out until he called me. I was so confused. I couldn't figure out what he was up to. And where the hell was Max!?

Luis did his research and brought me red lingerie and heels that were so high I couldn't even walk. I looked in the mirror and did not recognize myself. I looked like a stripper. The outfit was so skimpy if I balled it up it would fit in my hand. It was a one-piece made from metallic material and I felt naked when I had it on. My entire back was bare except for the tiny string that acted as a thong. In the front two skinny strips formed the letter V barely covering my tits and crotch. If I so much as blinked, the fabric shifted, and my tits popped out. I was way too chesty for this! I debated whether I looked foolish or hot. I heard Luis call my name through the door and I told him I wasn't so sure I wanted to come out. He coerced me to let him see the outfit. I slowly opened the door and his jaw practically dropped. I guess I looked hot.

Out of respect Luis didn't want to touch me until Max arrived. He handed me a black satin blindfold and told me to lie on the bed. Waiting. Vulnerable. Powerless. My mind raced wondering what was going to happen. Am I going to love this or regret it? After an eternity there was a knock on the door and I heard Max's voice. And so it began.

Max and I had had sex before, but we were simpler. It was straightforward. Never outfits or toys or bells and whistles. Luis, however, was a whirlwind of paraphernalia and fetishes and kinkiness. I had never experienced pleasure to that degree in my life. Luis assumed leadership and orchestrated the different scenarios and positions but was careful not to overshadow Max and was conscious of how much time each got to spend with me.

At one point when Max was fucking me, Luis put his hand over my face, covering my mouth and nose. My hands were bound but I was no longer blindfolded. I was so terrified at first, but when Luis looked in my eyes, I had complete faith in him. I didn't know him, but he had this aura. Dominant yet caring. Rough yet tender. So complex. I couldn't comprehend why I was allowing this breathing depravation yet I loved it. I had an incredible orgasm, and in that second, I knew he was going to be a special person. I am normally a dominant female but I was submissive to him.

We explored bondage, we played with toys, and we conquered DV. I was riding Luis and I heard him tell Max to join in. Max approached from behind and I leaned my body forward. I kissed Luis as Max slid his cock inside me, on top of Luis's. The addition of another penis was so effortless. I had expected it to be more cumbersome. I can't even

Chapter 15. Limo Luis

describe how hot having two guys inside me was. I was so proud of myself. I was a champion.

Later I blew Max and he came in my mouth. I crawled over to Luis and kissed him with Max's cum in my mouth. It was unbelievably raunchy. Luis was so turned on he flipped me over and fucked me extra hard. The entire night I was staring at his eyes and felt this electric connection. For hours, we all fucked like animals. None of us had any energy left so we relaxed in the room and chatted.

Luis wanted me to keep the outfit and heels as a gift. How sweet. Then he gave me a dozen red roses he had hidden in a shopping bag to thank me for allowing him the pleasure of joining us. We went directly to the diner, having worked up our appetites. The three of us sat in a booth and talked about what had just happened. We were sharing our favorite parts and agreed we made an awesome trio. We were still hyped up from our escapades, and our voices grew increasingly louder and other patrons could hear our conversation. We got strange looks, but we didn't care. In the parking lot I retrieved two small white boxes from my car and handed one to Luis and one to Max. They held cupcakes I had made as a sign of appreciation for them planning this evening for me.

The next day I was still thinking about Luis. I needed to see him again. As good as it was as a threesome I sensed there was something deeper between us. Since respect was important, we asked Max who introduced us if we had his permission to play alone, and he granted it. We planned a private date soon after.

Luis was coming to visit me. At 7:45, I texted him a casual "Are we still on for 8?" His response was "Don't question me. Now I will be there at 8:30." Who does this guy think he is? What an obnoxious thing to say. He must have mistaken me for a submissive girl. For some reason I replied, "Fine." I planned to give him a piece of my mind the minute I saw him. If any other guy spoke to me that way, I would tell him to fuck off. But Luis was different.

Headlights shone in my driveway and I stormed outside. I was flabbergasted to see a shiny black limousine. The passenger window lowered and a shadowy figure said, "What are you waiting for? Get in, girl." I cautiously got in. Luis was leaning against the driver side window and said, "Hello." "What's up?" I asked with an edge in my voice. "Are you angry that I am late?" "I value punctuality. I don't appreciate when people waste my time." Luis looked at me. "I'm not wasting your time. I was proving a point." "Oh, and what was that?" I asked with some sassiness. "You need to trust me. If I say I will be here, I will be here. Without trust, we cannot do the things I have planned for you." A valid explanation, I thought. My follow-up question was why on Earth were we in a fucking limo?!

Luis owned a limousine company. Outfitted with colorful lights and music, heat and A/C, a cooler with drinks, the limo had everything you needed to be a mobile sex machine—it was fucking brilliant! He literally just parked the limo on a main road in a busy downtown area full of restaurants and bars. The sidewalks were bustling with couples and families out for the evening. I wasn't so sure this was a good idea, but Luis told me to chillax. He did this all the time. The windows were tinted so we were fine.

I laid on the make-shift bed and had a hard time focusing on him. I was distracted by the footsteps and voices of the people walking by. Once his mouth was on my pussy the background noise faded. It was just him and me. Our first time alone was so powerful. The intensity and chemistry were unbearable. His main pleasure was my pleasure. Every girl's dream. Every touch was acutely intentional; every kiss was meaningful. We fed off each other's energy. We fucked for hours. I was exhausted and sweaty. I really had to pee, so Luis handed me an empty Big Gulp cup and baby wipes. I scrunched my face at him and hesitated. He reached his hand out further and said, "What are you waiting for? Just pee in the cup." For a moment, I wanted to tell him I was too classy to pee in a cup in a car but realized that might sound ironic after everything else he had seen me do. So I grabbed the cup, squatted over it and emptied my bladder. It wasn't awkward at all. After, Luis cracked the door open and emptied the cup along the curb. He said, "Let's keep the cup in case you need to go again." I shrugged. "Good idea." That was the beginning of a true friendship.

Luis bought me breakfast. I inhaled the special with eggs, bacon, pancakes and sausage. Luis just watched me. I was like a homeless child who hadn't eaten in weeks. We became fast friends. We met every few days. Being with him was an alternate reality. His biggest turn on was sharing me/fucking me after other guys did (used pussy). To outsiders, it may seem like he was using me or mistreating me but it was the complete

Chapter 15. Limo Luis

opposite. He gave me permission to be free and uninhibited with zero judgment. He was my sexual fairy godmother—my own personal genie, devotedly granting any wish. Shame did not exist between us and that was a foreign concept to me. In a world where most guys made me feel insignificant, Luis fed me confidence and made me feel invincible. His motto was "Women are flowers that need to blossom to their full potential, but most guys just trample them and tear out their petals." He reminded me, "You are the queen bee and they are here to serve you." "They are the tools—not you." "They can't handle you. You are superior to them. They don't understand what to do with someone of your caliber." Luis undoubtedly helped Scarlet transform into the beautiful beast she was meant to be.

We went from 0 to 100 in no time. Each adventure was more extreme and daring than the previous. He compared me to a hermit crab and nicknamed me "Shelly." So perfect. As bold as Scarlet was, occasionally my shy vanilla self momentarily resurfaced. I had a thick, tough shell, a guarded exterior. I might be slow to poke my head out, waiting until I felt safe, and I could retract in an instant when threatened. I avoided confrontation as best I could, but when I was pushed too far, my claws were my last resort and I would attack with no mercy. Luis referred to himself as "the Dominican Dynamite" because he would light the fuse and watch the explosion. I called him "Hulk." He was a massive, explosive beast. Larger than life. Eighth Wonder of the World. "What we have is a rare and special thing. We have done more than most ever will," he'd say.

It was like a dream. The dynamic between Luis and me was so incredibly peculiar. How much could I turn the other person on? What lengths would I go to? What was the benefit in return? Who technically had the power? Our relationship had a monumental impact on me and forced me to question many things. It was an emotional, physical and mental journey for me. Emotionally, why am I doing this? What is wrong with me? I was raised in a normal family so why am I so fucking deviant? I was never raped or molested so where did these aberrant fantasies come from? How much abuse could my body handle physically? How many people could I fuck and in what combinations? How hard could I get fucked? I was into rough sex so how hard could you hit me/choke me/pull my hair before you broke me? Could I mentally convert pain to pleasure? Could I turn doing something I didn't want to do into pleasure because I see how much my partner loves it? Could I be submissive when it went against every fiber in my stubborn body?

Sometimes Luis would pick me up just after I fucked another guy and ravage me. Luis got so hard licking other guys' cum off my body; the fresher the better. Other times we hit the town. One of our favorite games consisted of me lying blindfolded in the back of the limo in lingerie. The limo would stop somewhere, the door would open and a man he carefully chose beforehand would get in. Luis would drive around while the mystery man and I played. Sometimes the partition was up and other times it was down so Luis could watch us in the rearview mirror.

The first time I never took the blindfold off because I was too paranoid to see who Luis chose. I felt the mystery man's face with my hand as a real blind person would. I came across a bald head and beard I did not like. I was always so ultra-picky about who I fucked; I had a type. Luis would always argue girls want the beautiful Ferrari but sometimes the beat-up Ford gets you there better and is more reliable. And he was right. Skill and looks are not directly related and personality goes a long way. This guy was a little too passive for me. I preferred aggressive guys. Luis had to keep telling him to touch me and use my body. We kissed and he started to loosen up. He fucked me and his cock was huge. He was so deep inside me. Then we reversed, and I fucked him, still blindfolded. It was an unusual experience because I am a visual person. The mystery of the unknown was wildly intriguing. The only negative aspect was I couldn't see Luis's face. I always loved staring at him while I was being bad. It was one of my favorite parts. When we were done fucking, he thanked me and kissed me on the cheek. He thanked Luis for inviting him and said he hoped to keep in touch. I never saw his face and I never met him again.

The second time I lifted the blindfold halfway through, and other times I lifted the blindfold immediately. It depended on my mood—was I feeling withdrawn or aggressive? Did I want to be submissive or exercise my dominance? Things intensified fast and before I knew it the girl who swore against anal was having anal blindfolded with strangers in the back of a limo and enjoying every second of the irony. We were in the limo with another mystery guy. We were fucking and suddenly

Chapter 15. Limo Luis

Luis told me to get on all fours. My stomach dropped. He can't be serious. He knows I'm not into anal and it is reserved for special guys. Luis offered the guy lube and told him to have fun. My jaw tightened and I ground my teeth. Is Luis testing me or is this about to happen? Why does he need to ruin a lovely evening?

Since I met Luis he had given me a secret safe word—banana. The minute I said it everything would stop. Even though Luis seemed to be in control I technically had the power to override him which essentially put me in control. As my exposed ass was in the air just waiting for this stranger to put his cock in me, I couldn't decide if I should say the word. My heart raced. It was too soon to tap out. I wasn't a quitter, but I was inquisitive. I was curious about what was about to transpire.

I felt a cold, slimy hand on my ass. The mystery man was preparing me with the lube. I made fists with my hands and curled my toes to brace for impact. The anticipation was the worst part. Expecting pain was almost worse than experiencing pain. The mattress shifted beneath me as he knelt on the edge. His two hands gripped either side of my ass. Luis coached him. Go slowly. He explained this was a special occasion and the guy should appreciate it because fucking me in the ass was a rare occurrence. Luis talked about me like I was a priceless statue in a museum or a vintage car in a garage. "Be gentle, don't damage her." He calmed me.

As the mystery man's cock slid into my ass I grunted. Holy shit. His dick was bigger than the other guys I had anal with. Whoa! I took deep Lamaze breaths. Luis told me what a good girl I was. For the first few minutes my body twitched every time the mystery man's dick pounded me. I wasn't sure if I was going to throw up. I spoke to myself internally. I told myself to loosen up and ignore the pain. Focus on the pleasure Luis is getting from watching. Know I will be rewarded. Once my body adjusted to the motion the pain dissipated and it became a neutral feeling. I didn't get pleasure, but I didn't have pain. That was progress. I could live with that. After, Luis fucked me so hard that the condom got lodged inside me for three days.

The next guy who entered the limo helped break me into DP. Double penetration is one penis in your ass and one in your vagina. I was a little more comfortable with anal by then. It was not my favorite thing in the world, but I trained my body to accept it instead of fight it. I was riding this random guy and Luis came up behind me and slid his cock in my ass. DP was fucking hot. The combination of a penis in two holes was much more pleasurable than just anal alone. I sort of liked it. Luis announced it felt so amazing the other guy needed to try it. So they switched positions and I got DPed again.

Eventually Luis brought me two guys for my first MFMM. They took turns going down on me and fucking me. We tried different arrangements of partners for DP. All the guys knew each other so we had a blast. That night one of the guys spontaneously came all over my face and Luis was so turned on he instantly came on my face as well. Another rule broken—twice in one shot, literally. And I didn't mind at all. Another mind-blowing event. They admired how insatiable I was. They were tired, but I still wanted more.

Luis and I attempted a few clubs together. Normally, as I mentioned, I do not partner as a couple, but this was different because we were only picking up single guys. Luis loved watching me be the center of attention. Every outing was unconventional, so I never knew what to expect. Luis had a collar and if he told me to wear it I had to do whatever he said; I had to obey. Without the collar, I was the alpha; I was in charge.

One Thursday night we were at a club. It was smaller and located on the third floor of a building. We had to walk up so many steps my calves were on fire because I was in heels. A bouncer welcomed us and immediately through the door we came to the check in counter. Luis gave our names, paid and handed over my coat. To the left was a small room with a bar where a handful of fully dressed folks mingled. To the right was a restroom and then another door leading to the main area. The foyer was tight with another restroom, a water cooler and cups on a small table. Rehydration station. A wall with a doorway but no door led to the actual play area. The room was extremely cramped with five large beds taking up most of the space.

We found mostly single guys, some dressed and some naked. They hovered over beds, drooling, praying for action. The space felt so claustrophobic and the energy was overwhelming. We sat on a little bench, which was the only seating in the room. I cuddled up against Luis and we just observed. The crowd was not very attractive and most of the people were not even in good shape. I grew anxious and fidgety and asked Luis to fuck me. Without saying a word, he shook his head no. I

Chapter 15. Limo Luis

pouted. "But I am horny." "You are a big girl. If you want to get fucked then make it happen," Luis responded casually. I was in charge, I guessed. A few minutes passed as I contemplated my choices. I leaned over, kissed Luis and declared, "I am going for a walk."

I followed my target, a young Spanish guy, to the water cooler and said, "Hello." He was fully clothed, wearing jeans and a blue sweater, which meant he hadn't fucked anyone else yet. I preferred to be the first. I didn't want to fuck a guy who had just fucked some filthy girl. Too unsanitary. He asked if I came here often and if I was alone. I said, "First time and I am with a date but free to play alone." Without any more questions, he invited me to have sex and I led the way back inside. Simple procedure. I stopped in front of Luis, put my hand out and said, "Condoms, please." He grinned and placed them in my palm. I directed my new companion to a bed and removed my dress. I had no intention of wasting time. We kissed briefly then he fucked me. It was decent, but I decided to get on top and rock his world. A crowd gathered, and when I looked up, Luis was sitting on the edge of the bed, so I reached over and squeezed his hand.

I fucked this boy a little longer until I was bored. With no warning or apology, I stopped and climbed off of him to straddle Luis. I kissed him hard and said, "Will you fuck me now?" He handed me my dress and said, "Let's go." Yes! I got what I wanted. He fucked me extra hard in the limo. He told me how hard his cock was as he watched me take advantage of that innocent boy. Then we found a diner and ate a huge breakfast and drank peanut butter milkshakes. I got home around 5 a.m. I slept for three hours, then went to work without showering. I was a zombie, but a happy zombie. I loved feeling dirty, covered in Luis' sweat and cum all day.

On our next visit to that club, I was in a feral hunting mood. My short red dress fit me like a glove and I felt too sexy not to get fucked. The club had been renovated. A wall had been removed which made the play area much bigger and, I felt, way more comfortable. I had room to breathe. I needed my personal space. As usual, no guys were my type and I was getting perturbed. I needed to cause trouble. We didn't drive all the way here to go home empty-handed. I was a professional at making a scene—I just needed to get creative.

My attention kept going back to a younger light-skinned black guy who looked like he lifted weights. Time to break some more rules. I turned to Luis and casually said, "What if I fuck that black guy? Would you like it?" He was so surprised but the look in his eyes was priceless. "Go for it." As soon as the words left my mouth, I regretted them. Fucking this guy was so beyond my comfort zone and I was stuck. I kept stalling. "I need a push," I said. Taking off my dress, I announced I was going to the restroom. When I returned, the black guy approached me and said, "Your friend told me to fuck you." And so he did. He was sweet and touched me like he was afraid of hurting me. He had no idea who he was dealing with. I was in beast mode. I ordered him to lie down and I fucked him good. His eyes were so wide as my body pounded against his. He screamed that he was about to cum and I smiled. He didn't last very long.

After, he politely thanked me for choosing him. Luis told me to get on all fours on the bed and that same night I fucked my second black guy. I never even saw his face until we were done. A crowd gathered to watch. The sex was terrible. It was uninspired and he had no rhythm. I stared at Luis, rolling my eyes as if to say I was disheartened with his choice. We both knew this display of obedience would lead to incredible limo sex and a killer breakfast as always.

On a visit to NYC—it was Luis's first time there and he wanted to make it unforgettable—I posted a Naughty Date, sifted through the applicants and chose one lucky winner. I gave Luis his number and I had no further contact with him. I savored the mystery. Normally we were parked somewhere when we played but Luis had a better idea. "Let's drive through Times Square while you two fuck in the back." "Okay, why not?" I was blindfolded in the back as the mystery man climbed in. When he kissed me, I got chills. We made out like savages and I ripped the blindfold off. I was so curious about him. I needed all my senses for this. I could tell Marcus was cute even in the dim lighting—light-skinned with a baby face and dimples.

The streets were congested with cars and cabs and tourists. We tried all the positions—me on top, him on top, him behind me. Pedestrians walked by the tinted windows, their faces literally just inches from mine. Only a thin piece of glass separated us. I was screaming loudly but the city was so noisy no one noticed. My hands slammed against the window as he fucked me. What a surreal experience. It was so thrilling. It was like having sex in public, but we were invisible. Marcus was on top of me and I could see all the lights and billboards pass by upside down through the open moon roof as I orgasmed. They became a blur of colors as my eyes rolled back and my eyelids closed. Luis videotaped us so we could watch it later. We were so fired up. What next? There was always another plan with Luis.

We went to a sex club and wasted no time engaging in a threesome on a public bed while everyone there watched. We were in our own world, oblivious to the other people. They were there to socialize; we were there to fuck. It was a precisely choreographed dance. I blew one while the other fucked me. Then they switched. One went down on me while I sucked the other one's dick or kissed him. Luis made me squirt so heavily that the onlookers gasped. A voice announced the club was closing in a few minutes, so everyone needed to leave. We quickly finished up and the sheets were soaked. There were hardly any dry spots on the queen-size mattress. I marveled at the mess we made. Several people congratulated me for taking such a good pounding. Someone complimented my underwear. We dressed and left. We were probably there for only an hour, but it was an hour well spent. We dropped Marcus off at the subway station and found a place to eat. What a trip!

One Sunday a few weeks later, I got a call from Luis. He said he had bought me a present and wanted to deliver it. He lived about an hour and a half from my condo. "Why aren't you spending the day with your family?" I asked. "I am, we are all coming," he replied. I had briefly met his wife, Elena, at a party I attended with Max a few weeks after our killer MFM. She was a gorgeous Italian with a short, fashionable haircut and an elegance about her. She was mellow and partied at a level three while Luis was off the charts. They had an enjoyable sex life but swinging allowed them to fill in the gaps. He encouraged Elena to fuck guys on the side so he could enjoy her used pussy. I had previously asked her permission to see Luis to prevent any drama. A few hours later, the entire family showed up and the kids (a 13-year-old daughter, an 11-year-old daughter and a seven-year-old son) attacked me with enormous hugs. They were dying to meet me because they had heard so much about me, aside from the sex parts. We hung out at my complex's pool where they met my vanilla neighbors and a few friends. It was freaking weird, but then not weird at all. The hard part was explaining who this family was and how I knew them. We lied, obviously. The younger daughter proudly presented me with my gift—a sterling silver necklace with the initial "C" in ruby gemstones. Nice!

After they had their fill of swimming, our crew went to lunch at a cafe a few blocks away. The kids asked me questions and filled me in on their hobbies and school-related activities. I treated them to gelato at the ice cream shop next door. We dawdled over to the pavilion and the kids hit the swing set while Elena and I chatted about her job. "Do you have anywhere you need to be right now?" Luis asked. I shook my head and then, catching on, said, "I bet I do now." He smiled and ordered everyone in the car pronto, saying we would be late. Elena drove while Luis squished himself in the backseat between the kids. The mystery location was a mini-golf course. So random but that's why I adored him. Always the unexpected. We spent the rest of the afternoon hitting balls and hanging out. I wondered if people thought I was Luis and Elena's niece, their daughter or their babysitter. I knew none of them would surmise I was the girl allowed to fuck this woman's husband whenever I wanted.

Being invited into someone's home life was uncommon and to be regarded as very special. Maybe in a sense it healed some of the scars from Elliot. Luis never hid me and never kept me at a safe distance from his real life. I always respected Luis's marriage and family, grateful for the time he spent away from them to be with me and never greedy. I would occasionally send him home with pastries for his family or send a Christmas card. I cared for his family because I cared for him.

Chapter 16

Scarlet Fever

End of April 2017

    I had been running hard for five months with Luis. I was a fire and he was the gasoline. I was rapidly spreading and burning out of control. Every week I needed more. More sex, more guys, crazier situations. My job was killing me. Due to a recent promotion, I was working seven days a week, underpaid and underappreciated. My attitude started changing due to the unbearable stress. I was always agitated and moody. Sleep was impossible because my mind raced constantly. Friends grew concerned about my health and sanity and encouraged me to find more balance in my life. Cutting back at work would be a failure in my eyes. The thought sparked the same emotions as leaving Elliot had years earlier. I could not accept defeat after all the sacrifices I had made. Quitting now meant all my efforts were wasted and I could not accept that. I needed an escape.

    I called Luis and asked him to plan something legendary, and so he did. I drove to the hotel where we first met. I was not okay. I was not myself. I needed this too much. I contemplated canceling our date but ignored the doubt and proceeded.

    I was on the bed blindfolded. The door opened and then a hand touched me. I snuck a peak and saw Tommy, one of my previous limo escapades. I was pleased to see him. Luis disappeared and Tommy and I enjoyed each other for a little while. My mood was lifting. I was glad I came after all. Tommy was a great kisser and I melted as he went down on me. Maybe this evening would be the cure I needed. About 20 minutes later, I was eagerly riding Tommy when Luis opened the door and directed me to put the blindfold back on. I was annoyed. I didn't feel like being told what to do, but, reluctantly, I did it. I heard several people enter the room and soft voices, but I couldn't understand the words. I was on display and felt edgy. Normally I loved being the center of attention in Luis's performances, but I knew I wasn't myself today. Shit. Maybe I should've stayed home. I usually lived for this stuff but not today. I tried to continue having sex with Tommy, but I couldn't focus. I was not connected.

Fingers lightly traced the length of my arm and I tensed. Tommy whispered in my ear: "Are you okay?" "I don't know," I answered. Something was different. The hand was small and soft and gentle. My jaw tightened as my nostrils flared. Fucking Luis. Infamous for his plot twists. Luis leaned in and brushed a piece of hair from my face. I quietly asked if that was a girl. He chuckled and replied, "Pretend it's a boy with small hands." Not funny. Bringing another girl outraged me and mocking me infuriated me more. Tommy was sweet. "Pretend it is just you and me. Just feel me." But I couldn't. I wanted to scream. I didn't know what to do. I felt vulnerable and paranoid, so I excused myself to the bathroom. I couldn't breathe. There was a knock on the door, but I didn't answer. I stared at myself in the mirror, trying to figure out what to do next. Cooperate or bail? Finally, I came out and told Luis I wasn't into this. He looked at me, confused. "You wanted this." I stared back, silent. I had never disobeyed him before. He was upset. I was angry. I got on the bed and we tried again. Maybe I could power through this. I climbed back on top of Tommy and slid his cock into me. I tried to fuck him, but I couldn't concentrate. I was lifeless. I kept starting and stopping. I rolled off of him and just laid there. I tried to shut my mind. I was not getting pleasure from this.

Luis leaned over the edge of the bed and asked if he could fuck me. "No." He was taken aback by my response. He asked again, and I said, "I'm not in the mood." Luis offered to tell the other girl to leave but that seemed even more embarrassing. I could imagine what would be said. I would be the crazy bitch who kicked some random girl out of a hotel room because I was supposedly jealous. I'd be a Unicorn diva. My body was tense like a corpse. I sat up and moved to the corner of the bed and told Luis I needed to go home. I couldn't be here. He collected my clothes and I faced the wall as I got dressed, never looking to see who else was in the room. We walked down the hall and rode the elevator to the

Chapter 16. Scarlet Fever

ground floor without exchanging a word. He walked me to my car and we disagreed about what happened. Luis claimed I was too stressed and overexhausted from working so much. I needed to get a grip. I insisted he damn well knew her presence would upset me. Why was he fucking with me? I got in my car and broke down. I cried hysterically.

Shame. I was mortified for ruining the night. I was the main attraction and all these people showed up to specifically fuck me. Luis tried to calm me down but eventually he went back to the hotel to deal with his guests and I went home. I cried and cursed the entire way. I was mad at him. I was mad at myself. We didn't speak for two weeks. He later apologized and said, "I honestly thought you wanted that. I had seven guys coming to fuck you, some old, some new; I was trying to spoil you. The other girl was simply there to lend a hand if you needed a break or to keep the guys entertained while they waited for their turn with you." Ugh. "I did not need back up. You knew for a fact I don't like playing with guys after girls I don't know did." I didn't like contaminated body parts. They reduced the sex appeal.

I apologized too, however, acknowledging I was not in the right frame of mind for that. Maybe Scarlet should've allowed Luis to remove the other girl so she could enjoy her fan club. Who knows? Too late now. We talked occasionally for a few weeks before we saw each other again. We finally hung out and it was nice to see him. The sex was great, but I still felt empty. I told him I needed to be alone for a while longer, nothing personal. I was damaged. Luis understood. "I will be there whenever you choose to come back." I think of him whenever I wear my beloved necklace.

Chapter 17

Reset

May 2017

    My meltdown at the hotel was a blaring signal. Maybe I was using a Band-Aid to treat myself instead of having surgery to remove the tumor. I removed myself from the Lifestyle because I was finally ready to settle down and date vanilla. I was in my 30s; it was time to grow up and get serious. I was tired of people interrogating me for still being single. How sad that I was alone. What was wrong with me that I couldn't find a man? I hid my profile and cut ties with all existing partners. I went back on Match.com and had seven terrible dates in a row. The guys were so dull. None of them were memorable. Pretending to be fascinated by unoriginal conversation drove me insane. Sometimes I wanted to stab myself with a fork just so I could feel something. But this was the real world. I had to disguise myself to fit into society. How else would I fool the vanilla public into believing I was one of them?

    Approaching an early mid-life crisis due to my job, I temporarily moved in with my mother. If you think living a double life was hard—try doing it in a two-bedroom condo with your mother hovering over you! It was a never-ending barrage of questions. Who are you going out with? When will you be home? Why are you always on your computer? What time are you going to work tomorrow? Privacy was nonexistent. I felt like I was back in high school. I sat in the bathroom with the faucet running when I spoke on the phone and changed clothes in my car. I tiptoed through the door in the middle of the night carrying my shoes so I wouldn't wake her. I wondered what she suspected I was up to.

Chapter 17. Reset

My friends advised me to seek guidance from a life coach. Ordinarily I would have laughed at the idea, but admitting I was lost was the first step to changing. My desperation was stronger than my indignity. I agreed—but kept quiet. I never thought this would be my life at 35. During my first session with the life coach, I filled out a questionnaire and rated specific aspects of my life from one to ten. Career ranked a one and love life registered a zero. My coach promised these numbers would rise within three months. I rolled my eyes and hoped I hadn't thrown my money away.

To my amazement, this stranger gave me the strength to take control of my life. Because she was a professional, accredited coach, her opinion carried more weight than those of my friends even though they were saying the exact same things. I accepted her recommendations like you would accept a prescription to treat an illness from a medical doctor. I did not argue; I just surrendered. I learned several of my closest friends had used coaches in the past and praised the experience. They assured me it was nothing to be embarrassed about and told me they were proud of me for seeking help. I was fortunate to have female friends who were intelligent, resilient, successful, independent, determined role models. They had dealt with their own burdens and bravely reinvented themselves, which inspired me to do the same. They commended me for choosing to abandon my miserable job and promised me the universe would lead me in the right direction. I need not worry. Just enjoy the journey.

My outlook changed, and although my coach did not technically make decisions for me, her giving me permission to make the changes I wanted gave me relief. It never occurred to me that I could alter my own path. I just accepted I was a chef and I would die a chef. Besides, who was I if I wasn't a chef? That was my identity. Wasn't it? With her support, I had the audacity to leave my job. Shedding my chef coat was as exhilarating as losing my bikini on the nude beach. It was a rebirth. Saying "My coach thinks I should quit my job" as opposed to saying "I quit my job" made me feel better. It sounded legitimate. I wasn't giving up; I was saving myself. It removed the guilt. I was dropping out of college all over again.

The first day I did not set an alarm or have anywhere to be was miraculous. A tremendous weight had been lifted off my shoulders and

I could finally relax. Free time was an unfamiliar concept. I was always rushing and following strict schedules and deadlines. For the first time in my life, I felt peaceful. My personality shifted from uptight and aggressive to laid-back and happy-go-lucky. In my new clear state, I adopted meditation and mindfulness. Living in the moment, focusing on positivity and renouncing negativity. I was more airy and outgoing. Until I figured out what my new career would be, I secured a part-time summer job on the beach. I earned enough to pay bills and afford gas. Sporting a golden tan, sun-kissed blonde highlights and a permanent smile, I honored myself by eating healthy, almost never drinking aside from an occasional glass of wine, sleeping better and working out religiously. My mind and body had never been stronger. I think this unfamiliar sensation was happiness. I scored my work situation an eight.

When we discussed my lack of a romance, my coach became the third person I disclosed my secret to, but we had a confidentiality agreement and I was paying her. How could she help me if she didn't know the entire truth? Instead of glossing over it, we scrutinized it. She suggested expressing my thoughts on paper could be restorative. That conversation coincidentally led to me writing this book. Once the pen hit the paper I was hooked—my latest fixation. Life is so mysterious—I never planned to be a chef, never intended to be a swinger, I never realized I could choose to stop being a chef, and I certainly never imagined I could be a writer. Funny the path your life takes unexpectedly. My life has been a compilation of accidental events and this is the first time I am the driver of the car instead of the passenger along for the ride. Maybe saying these things out loud will help me understand and heal myself. It might even help another woman in my position know she is not alone. I do not claim to be a superb writer. My words may not be eloquent, and my sentences may not be sophisticated, but they are authentic. I hope my honesty and rawness make me relatable and compensates for my literary shortcomings. This is not some fictional romance fantasy novel. This is my existence.

I hadn't had sex in 34 days. I sound like someone in AA counting her days of sobriety. For me, that was a long stretch, considering in my active phases I fucked several people a week, or even multiple guys in a day. Although I made a conscious decision to be temporarily celibate, my body was having side effects. Like going from drinking five cups of coffee a day to zero, I was jittery and my brain was a little hazy. I was like a vampire who hadn't had blood in a while. I wrote non-stop to distract myself from the withdrawals. I started to feel mentally cleansed.

Chapter 18

Resurrection

July 2017

    I reactivated my swinger profile because I severely missed it. Going from a long period in the vanilla world to re-entering the swinging world required me to hit a reset button in my brain. I needed to prepare mentally as I changed personas. I needed to exude poise and sex appeal. I needed to be stable emotionally so that I could make clear, safe, correct decisions for myself and I didn't end up doing things I regretted or putting myself in harmful situations. I needed to be in control and put myself first. I have realized that I can only swing when I am happy and choose to do it. If I do it out of loneliness or desperation, it always has negative results—like going to the supermarket when you are starving. You make irrational purchases, then go home and stuff your face with a bunch of junk food that instantly satisfies your craving but a few hours later leaves you with a stomachache and hating yourself. Whenever I did go back, meeting the first date was always nerve wracking. Did I remember what to do? But it was like ripping off a Band-Aid or riding a bike. Once that first kiss happened, a switch flipped. I dove in, and before I knew it, my alter ego took over and I was an animal. All the fears and doubts subsided and Scarlet was alive.

Lenny (NSA)

    I was in a great frame of my mind and my regular social life was flourishing but I was getting the urge for something more scandalous. After a few days online, there were no candidates jumping out at me. I

Chapter 18. Resurrection

patiently waited. I received an email from a guy with a lovely picture of his abs and noticed he had emailed me six times previously, but I had never responded. He seemed polite and reliable, so we started chatting, exchanged numbers and texted. We planned to meet for drinks a few nights later.

Sunday night came and it was game time. We were supposed to meet at 7 but he was running late due to traffic. I paced around my living room waiting for his text saying he was close. I never get dressed until the last minute. At almost 8, he gave me the 15-minute warning. I threw my clothes on, including a pair of shorts I had recently bought without trying on which turned out to be inappropriately short for most occasions but suitable for a Lifestyle date. The bar was close so I walked—the entire time second-guessing my attire, constantly touching my ass to see how short my shorts were and paranoid my ass cheeks were visible as I walked. I got a lot of attention from guys passing by.

I arrived at the bar first, sat down and got a glass of water. I was anxious. What if I hated him? Lenny walked in and I was relieved. Mid-30s, good looking, bald head, muscular, tattoo on his arm, nice, friendly energy. We ordered two Blue Moons and instantly hit it off. It felt like a vanilla date—we talked about work and friends and the like. Then we shifted to juicier conversation. Lenny was respectful, nothing graphic, mostly how we got involved and how long we had been swinging. After the second beer, I excused myself to go to the restroom and he told me how much he liked my shorts and how sublime my ass looked. I laughed. That boosted my confidence.

I returned and thought, "Let's do this before I chicken out." "Are you ready to go?" I asked. "Sure," Lenny said. I got in his car and he drove to the hotel conveniently located one mile away. After he checked us in, we grabbed another drink from the lobby bar and headed upstairs.

The room was nice. I had never been to this hotel before. I always went to the bathroom right away to freshen up, give myself a pep talk. I stepped out in my red lacy bra and panties and joined Lenny on the bed. We started to kiss, and I was immediately comfortable. I was back in business. Lenny had amazing skills and I was squirting all over the place, so the sheets were totally soaked within minutes. We had great sex, he had a nice-sized cock and he was super hard. A few hours later, we got dressed and he drove me home.

We texted sporadically over the next few days, reliving the fun. I asked if he was into threesomes/MFM and he enthusiastically said, "Absolutely!" He mentioned he had a potential guy, so he gave me his friend's profile and I checked him out. He was in his late 20s (I generally don't meet younger guys), very cute and married but he played separate. The fact Lenny vouched for him went a long way, so I said, "Let's meet tonight. I am bored." We briefly texted each other to get acquainted. We couldn't make that night work so we planned to meet late the following Saturday when we were done with our own vanilla friends and lives.

At 12:30 Lenny texted me they were together and on their way. I said goodbye to my friends and met them in the hotel parking lot at 12:45. The hotel, unfortunately, was full. "Aren't you guys prepared? You had all day to make a reservation." I shook my head and mocked them. The second hotel was also full. I was getting tired and losing interest, but we were determined to do this. The third time was a charm. We scored a room! We parked both cars and I was finally introduced to my future sex partner. He was adorable but quiet. The three of us got in the elevator and I said, "Thanks for coming out." As usual I made a beeline for the bathroom. It was late, after 1 in the morning, and I had work the next day. I got bold and came out in my black bra and stringy thong.

They were both fully dressed on the bed watching an old episode of *South Park*. I crawled between them and nothing happened. Hmmm … do I need to do everything? I leaned over and kissed Lenny and he grabbed my ass. Then nothing. I sat up, restless. "Why is everyone so goddamn shy?" They looked at each other and then it was showtime. I started sucking Lenny's cock while his friend went down on me. They were quiet; there wasn't much talking. Lenny's friend was timid, and I was too aggressive for him, I think. We tried different positions and arrangements. I hadn't had a MFM recently which made it fun. In between the sex Lenny made me squirt. His friend had the softest jumbo marshmallow lips. I liked kissing him. It was now 3 in the morning so the night abruptly ended. They left, politely thanking me for the pleasure, and I slept scrunched on the corner of the bed in the only dry spot.

Chapter 18. Resurrection

Charlie (NSA)

After that meet went so well I was ready for more. I clicked on a profile I had seen a million times. The guy had been emailing me for literally two years. We had exchanged a few messages, but I was never ready to meet. Not sure why. He just wasn't what I was looking for. For reasons unknown to me, now I was interested. I emailed him, and he was beyond surprised to hear from me, but he was still keen to hang out. He lived 20 minutes from me all along, but of course, now that I want to fuck him, he was living an hour away.

We texted and I was intrigued by the good conversation, flirty and sexy but not rude. Eventually we spoke on the phone and I could sense the energy and attraction; there was a lot of laughing and joking. He was confident but not arrogant. Now I wanted to meet him. Our schedules were opposite so coordinating seemed impossible. We made plans a few times, but they always failed. I was getting impatient. I hated waiting. I wanted him now. I had to get creative. I hated meeting new people during the day because the vibe was different. You had to be bolder since you couldn't have a drink or wear a sexy dress. There was more pressure and I didn't feel as sexy. But I decided to take a chance. Monday, 10 a.m.—meet at the hotel with no introduction first. Ugh, the stress (for me, at least)! What if I get there and am not attracted? How can I leave right away without being a bitch?

That morning he texted me the room number: 415. I was in tight black yoga pants, a tank top and sneakers. As I walked down the hallway, I applied more deodorant because I was afraid my nerves would make me sweaty. I cracked my knuckles and knocked on the door. Charlie opened it and he looked true to his picture. He was light-skinned and had a goatee, and he was wearing a white t-shirt, gray sweatpants, bright yellow Nike sneakers and a gold chain with a cross. He had a wide smile and I felt at ease. We said hello and I went to the bathroom to gather myself. Uncharacteristically, I emerged still fully dressed. I blushed and said, "This is super awkward" as I avoided eye contact. Charlie laughed. I could be really goofy before I got into the zone. He was lying on the bed and reached his hand out for mine. I took it and knelt on the bed.

Charlie sat up and kissed me. Good kisser. Charlie grabbed my hair. I loved that. He was just aggressive enough. I could feel his desire.

My shirt came off and he kissed my breasts. I rubbed my hand over his smooth bald head and noticed a scar towards the nape of his neck. I enjoyed kissing him. He gently put me down on my back and my pants and underwear came off at once. I thought, "Really? You didn't even notice my expensive panties?" Boys…. Okay, I refocused on his mouth and hands all over me. His chain felt cold against my inner thigh as he went down on me. I was so turned on. He made me squirt and I adored him. A huge snake tattoo coiled around his left arm. We fucked for a while. Him on top, behind, me on top. We were very compatible. He was Mexican and kept telling me he loved my fat white girl ass. My fingers glided over a scar on his left ribs. He made me squirt before he entered me each time so it was super wet and slippery.

In between rounds we talked and laughed. He handed me a bottle of water and a wet towel to clean up. He was sweet and considerate. Charlie had to go to work so playtime was over. We showered together and he washed me off. In the parking lot, we joked it was unquestionably worth waiting two years for and I gave him a high five.

Tommy (FWB with Extreme Intimacy)

Tommy and I had a checkered history. I originally met him in the limo during the MFMM. He was just coming back from California on a red-eye and due to extreme jet lag was not on his A-game. The sex was subpar, but his oral skills were phenomenal, and he had a great personality, so I didn't mind. The next day he emailed me and pledged to make it up to me. The second time we crossed paths was at the infamous hotel room. He was the guy I was fucking when I had my temper tantrum. We had two strikes against us and I told him I thought the universe was against us having sex. We kept in touch and vowed to one day have sex.

Out of the blue, he invited me to his house along with Miguel (another limo patron) and Luis but neither was available. This was a big night—a rematch between two professional fighters. In reality, Tommy and I hardly knew each other. We had limited interactions. On the drive to his house, I wondered what would happen. It would either be another epic failure or spectacularly awesome. I hoped for the latter.

Chapter 18. Resurrection

I pulled into the driveway and he greeted me with a warm hug. I was walking behind him when he suddenly stopped and said, "I just realized I have been with you twice, yet I have never seen you walk ... or stand ... or dressed." Hysterical. Such a swinger thing to say! Having sex made you feel like you knew each other even though you technically didn't.

I had come straight from the gym, so I showered quickly and put on a blue bra and panties. Being so comfortable around him didn't seem strange; I guess our common link to Luis made us seem familiar. We kissed in the middle of the living room and he slapped my ass. We formally introduced ourselves as I surveyed my surroundings. Tommy, one of seven children, was an Irish software developer, stood 5'11", and had light brown hair and eyes and a gigantic Celtic cross on his muscular calf. Judging from the books on his shelf and the deer head over his mantle, I inferred he was a history buff and hunter.

A large flat-screen TV was tuned to a soft, sultry R&B station while images of sexy, shadowy silhouettes danced to the music. A full bar with chrome chairs and a Jacuzzi in his master bath completed this bachelor pad. "Are you ready for makeup sex?" "Oh no," I replied. "This is payback sex, sweetie. We both have a lot to prove." I laid on the lush king-sized bed adorned with a deer in the wilderness-themed comforter (which also supported my hunter theory) and he kissed me. He smelled fresh and I couldn't decipher if he wore cologne or deodorant.

He pulled me on top of him and we started to grind as we made out. He unhooked my bra and bit my nipples lightly. Soon my panties came off as he placed me on my back. He went down on me like he was enjoying his favorite meal. Oral utopia. I was directed to tilt my hips up and arch my back, and I knew where this was headed. He stuck several fingers inside me and used his other hand to press down on my stomach below my belly button. Pressure built until I was a volcano about to erupt. I screamed from the orgasm but was dry still. I was puzzled. Maybe I hadn't had enough water. Tommy lifted his cupped hand and poured my warm cum all over my body. It ran down my stomach and across my tits. The deer and I were soaked. That was a new twist on an old favorite and I was so fucking turned on. Tommy leaned over and licked my cum off me. Sexy!

We proceeded to make up for any previous shortcomings. Doggy-style, missionary, more squirting, sideways. He used coconut oil for lube and our bodies were a greasy mess. He announced he wanted anal. Those four ominous letters. Ugh. I did not respond so Tommy said, "Don't tell me you aren't into it—I saw what you did in that limo." I burst out laughing. Busted! I admitted I was rusty because I hadn't tried it in a while. He promised to be gentle, so I said okay. I curled up in a ball on my stomach and rested my face on a pillow. He inserted a small dildo in my ass and fucked me vaginally while I held a vibrator on my clit. I passed the first stage and we moved onto a larger dildo. "Still OK?" he checked. "Yes, I am." The third stage was his cock. I was so relaxed by then he could glide right in. As he pumped his cock in and out, he asked if I liked it. I said, "We are all good." "But do you like it? Because I don't want to just do it for my sake if you hate it." "I am just not used to it, but I am really OK," I replied, so we continued and settled into a rhythm. "Do you mind if I take the condom off and cum in your ass?" Tommy asked. "Sure, why not?" I shrugged. It felt right. He removed his condom and re-entered my ass raw and moaned loudly, telling me how incredible it felt as he came. We had fucked like crazy for more than an hour. We needed a break.

We grabbed a beer and chilled in the Jacuzzi before round two began. It was soon followed by round three. There was not a dry spot on the bed and I was dehydrated from losing so much fluid. We high fived and reveled in our success. We did not miss the people who did not show up and were psyched we got to be alone.

Tommy commanded my attention. We texted throughout the days and the conversation ranged from casual to sexy with a lot of sarcasm and laughter. The Friday after our first date we had a spontaneous second date. Tommy said he was excited for our last-minute plans and that made me feel good, wanted. Just like the time before, I drove to Tommy's and we spent the night switching from the hot tub to the bed. We got along so easily and we had fun whether we were fucking or just talking. We were also both cuddly. As I left, he said, "See you Monday." "I thought this was in place of Monday," I replied. Tommy scowled. "But I was really looking forward to seeing you again." "Didn't you have a rule about seeing a girl more than once in a week? That would be three times for us in eight days." Tommy assured me he didn't care, so I agreed.

My mind was already filled with questions. Did he like me? Was

Chapter 18. Resurrection

this how he treated all the girls he fucked? Did he just think I was so fun and easy-going we could get together without catching feelings? I dreaded the fact that I was going to need him to explain his motivation at some point. I needed to be up front about his intentions so I could avoid confusion.

Date three turned into a two-day escapade with Tommy. A mini-vacation filled with sex, the pool, the hot tub and food. I needed this. We had crazy fuck sessions and then personal conversations about our lives and why we were in the Lifestyle. I was fascinated when Tommy told me he mostly had swinger friends. He didn't have to lie or avoid situations or questions like I did, and I was slightly jealous that he was at peace. I asked how his relationships were with other single girls, and like every other guy I asked, he said it was different with me. While this was not real dating, the energy I put out made him want to have a deeper connection with me.

Tommy broke his arm playing football, so I headed to his house to play nurse. While I was driving, Luis happened to call just to say hi. I mentioned I was on my way to visit Tommy, who conveniently lived a few miles away from Luis. Luis told me he was free for the rest of the evening in case we wanted him to come by. "The guy literally broke his arm a few hours ago. Let's calm down," I suggested. "Tommy is a kinky fuck like me, so call me later," Luis replied.

I let myself in at Tommy's and gave him a careful hug and a soft kiss. His left arm was in a cast and he had no feeling from his shoulder to his fingers. I handed him a bag with get-well goodies—a stuffed teddy bear, chocolate bars and his favorite mint chocolate chip ice cream. He told me I was adorable and gave me a long thank you kiss. Our kisses had become very intimate, filled with emotion. He updated me on his morning at the hospital and I mentioned speaking with Luis. When he ordered me to remove my panties and sit on the edge of the couch I laughed and dismissed him. "Calm down, tiger." He looked at me quite seriously and said, "Panties off, now." "If you insist," I answered. This boy *is* crazy!

As instructed, I undressed, braced my ass on the edge of the couch and leaned back. Tommy wasted no time diving into my pussy. He told me he missed it as he inserted the fingers of his working hand inside me. In between moans, I complained, "This feels amazing but now I am super horny and can't even fuck you." Tommy looked up, confused. "Who said that?" I told him he needed to be careful. I didn't want to injure him. He pulled his wet hand out of my throbbing pussy and dried it on his shorts. He picked up his phone and typed a short message. Then he looked up at me. "Luis is coming over, so if I can't fuck you, at least he can." Then his mouth was back on my pussy. I closed my eyes and smiled.

After about 20 minutes, Tommy was satisfied and allowed me to get dressed. We cuddled on the couch and watched a documentary on Netflix while we ate pizza. I propped a bunch of pillows under his arm. His phone beeped. Tommy said Luis would be there at seven. I nodded, and we turned our attention back to the documentary about sex robots and the guys who love them. We were totally judging these guys. Talk about the pot calling the kettle black!

At 7:15, Tommy teased, "Your boy is late. He is delaying our play time." I furrowed my brow. "Is there a law we have to wait?" He reached down and released his cock from his shorts and I put it in my mouth. As I was blowing him, I heard a door open and footsteps coming toward us. I lifted my head and there was Luis; I hadn't seen him in four months. He was standing behind the couch, so I stood on the cushion backward to face him. I reached over and gave him a massive hug. "Lovely to see you, stranger," I said as I kissed him on the lips. "Good to see you too, girly girl." This was going to quite a reunion.

The three of us chatted briefly and then Tommy got up to go take his clothes out of the dryer. Luis undressed, walked over and stood in front of me as I sat on the couch. He tugged on my arm. "Stand so I can get a look at you." It had been so long. I obediently stood in front of him and I sensed being with him would be just like old times. "Turn around." As I did, he pushed my back, causing me to fall forward. I bent at my knees and my hands grabbed the top of the couch. He slapped my ass and I flinched—and smiled. I could see Tommy folding laundry through the doorway ahead of me. His eyes caught mine momentarily, then he went back to the towel he was folding. Luis removed my panties then licked his hand and rubbed my pussy through my legs. He shoved his hard cock deep inside me and I let out a sigh of relief. I missed him. He pounded me as he grabbed me by the back of the neck.

Tommy finished his chore and rejoined us in the living room. Luis

Chapter 18. Resurrection

extracted his dick, lightly slapped my ass and said, "Let's go to the bed. You too, Tommy." I scurried to the bed and climbed on. "Where do you want me?" I remembered Tommy was currently disabled, although he sure didn't act that way, so Luis and I arranged a few pillows so he could lie comfortably on his back. Once he was set, I crawled over and kissed him. Then I sucked his cock. A few minutes passed and I didn't feel Luis near us. I flipped over and laid on my back between Tommy's legs with my head rested on his inner thigh. I reached one arm above my head and stroked his cock softly as I stared at Luis. With my other hand, I wiggled my fingers at him. Luis could read my mind. He slipped his hand into my pussy and moved it violently in an effort to make me squirt. The orgasm was out of this world, but I didn't feel the customary spray of fluid that Luis was known for creating. Luis wiped his soaking wet hand across my face and said sarcastically, "Oh not good enough for you?" as he laughed. These boys and their tricks! Dirty fucker. I loved him.

Luis returned to his post on the couch and I resumed fucking Tommy, my poor invalid. Tommy read my mind and shouted for Luis to join us. I looked behind me. "It's making me anxious not knowing what you are doing. I think you are plotting something." "I am just watching. Take care of Tommy. Be a good girl," Luis laughed. When he was ready, Luis moved closer and reached between my legs and touched my clit. "Welcome to the party," I said.

I leaned sideways and kissed Luis. Now we were all together. Luis asked if we were ready for DP and DV. "DV!" I shouted. Luis chuckled. "I know you love that." Tommy had never tried DV and was against it. He thought it was too personal to have another dick on his. Luis told me to fuck Tommy to get warmed up. I was riding Tommy as I hard as he wanted me to, but I was worried about hurting his arm. He didn't care but I did. I was paranoid. I kept leaning down to kiss him. He softly whispered, "I'll do DV." I squinted. "We don't need to. It's not a big deal." "I know you love it," Tommy said. "But I know you don't," I tried to argue. "I don't want to force you." He gazed into my eyes and said, "I want to do this for you." I stopped fucking him and looked at him intently. "Why?" "I want to make you happy," he replied. "I guess I really like you." I grabbed his face with both hands and kissed him so hard. Most girls get flowers or jewelry from their gentleman—but I got another dick!

I sat straight up and slowly started to ride him again as I stared into his eyes. There was a strong connection. I reached one arm behind my back and wiggled my fingers at Luis. "Come, Luis, we are ready for you." As Luis moved closer to us I proudly announced, "Tommy is ready for his first DV." Luis knelt behind me and told Tommy to close his legs and me to widen mine. I put my face close to Tommy's and asked once more, "Are you ready?" "Yes." As I fucked Tommy I used my elbows to brace my body and keep my weight of his chest and arm. I felt Luis's cock enter me and I let out a half laugh, half scream as I told him he was in the wrong hole. "Oh, shit, is that your ass?" "Yes!" I shouted. "OK, well I guess we are starting with DP," Luis responded. "Ahhh, OK, fine." "Don't worry," he assured me. "We will switch back and forth." "Well you could've at least used some lube," I said, and Luis replied, "Honey, trust me, you are wet enough on your own."

After a few minutes of DP Luis was ready to alternate. As he put his dick in my pussy, I whispered in Tommy's ear, "Just think about me." "I am." We kissed more. Sharing a new experience with someone was significant, especially if it was something he never planned to do. Tommy trusted me and made a sacrifice to please me. He was never going to forget I was the girl he shared his first DV with. Our threesome continued as Luis determined what combination we were in. Both guys talked dirty, calling me their good little slut and their filthy whore. They talked about me as if I wasn't there. Male bonding at its best. I was so turned on. During our last round of DP Luis came in my ass.

Luis removed himself and our trio returned to a duo as I fucked Tommy. Luis chilled on the bed a few inches away from us and suggested Tommy cum in my pussy so both holes could be filled with cum. I was their cum dumpster. That may sound offensive to some people, but with us, it was a compliment, a term of endearment of sorts. Tommy said, "No. I want you to do something I saw in a porn." I replied, "Oooh, I sense some payback for the DV. What can I do for you?" Tommy's request was that I take turns riding both their cocks, jumping back and forth between them. I grinned. "Your wish is my command." I motioned for Luis to scoot closer to us. I continued fucking Tommy until he told me to fuck Luis and so on. We rotated five or six times, then, during my last turn with Tommy, he came inside me. Mission accomplished.

I rolled off him and laid on my back, wiggled my foot at Luis. Let's

Chapter 18. Resurrection

see if he remembers my signals. He did. He walked over as Tommy got up to get a towel. Luis bent down and ate my pussy. He devoured me, sucking all of Tommy's cum out of me. Then he kissed me so I could taste myself. He pulled his face away from mine and gave me a devilish smirk. "I missed you so much," I said, meaning it.

Exhausted, we regrouped in the living room to drink bottled water and rehydrate.

Except for the fact that we were naked, and had just had a threesome, the vibe was that of any normal friends getting together to bullshit about life and work. Luis sat on a chair while I curled up next to Tommy on the couch and we held hands. Around 10:30, Luis left, and Tommy and I resumed our Netflix watching as if nothing had happened. I grabbed the pint of ice cream and one spoon and fed us both.

When we were ready to sleep, I again surrounded him with pillows on the couch. He told me he had a fun night and I agreed. I noted it was an unusual chemistry because when we met, Luis and I were the couple and Tommy was the additional guy. Now it was the opposite—Tommy and I were the couple and Luis was the additional guy. Equally fun experiences but a different twist. Tommy had a rock-hard erection even though he was half-asleep. He wanted me to fuck him, but I refused. "I think you had enough physical activity for just having broken your arm." He grimaced and went to sleep.

I sprawled out in the giant bed covered in sweat and fluids from three people. I set my alarm for 6:30 to give us an hour before I had to leave for work. When the alarm buzzed I gently woke Tommy and helped transport him and his pillows to the bed. I wanted to cuddle with him. He put my hand on his cock. Unbelievable! Completely hard already. I assumed the position and fucked him as he desired. He begged me to cum all over him, so I did. Several times. We checked the clock and were 30 minutes into our hour, so he said, "I want to fuck you from behind. I'm not sure if I can but I want to try." I dismounted him and bent over. As he fucked me, I asked, "Are you going to cum for me, baby?" He said he didn't think he could right now. "What about if you fuck my ass?" Tommy was intrigued. Knowing I don't love anal, he said, "Are you sure?" "Yes, you deserve it, sweetie," I replied. "You were so good to me last night." That was our form of give and take. Like telling your husband, you did the laundry, so I'll vacuum. Without any more discussion, he entered my ass and I gritted my teeth. We started slowly at first and then picked up momentum. He came hard and I smiled. I never liked to leave my partner unsatisfied. It was impolite.

I finally grabbed a much-needed shower and quickly dressed. Tommy walked me to the door and kissed me good-bye. Then, as only a swinger could, he said, "Don't forget to take your birth control today because I don't want to end up on Maury Povich battling with Luis over the paternity of a threesome baby." I had to call Max and tell him this insane story!

(By midday, the painkillers wore off and Tommy was in excruciating pain, but he claimed our rendezvous was worth it!)

Chapter 19

A Potential Peter

September 2017

    History was repeating itself. Tommy and I became inseparable and our situation resembled that of mine and Peter's. We were way too close. We texted 24/7 and hung out as much as possible. He cooked me dinner, escorted me to the nude beach and showered me with affection. We could easily be confused for a real couple and that frightened me because I didn't want to get hurt again.

    I couldn't tell if this would develop into anything more serious. It felt like we were on the verge of falling for each other, yet I didn't want to make assumptions. The old me would have to solve this mystery immediately and force results. The current me was curious but wanted to let it unfold organically so I remained open but cautious. As they say, you learn from history.

    The advantage I had now was that my vanilla girlfriends knew about my secret life. Amy and Marcy let me vent my discontent as well as boast my success with no judgment. They talked about their vanilla boyfriends and I talked about my various Lifestyle partners. I was now equally included in our friendship. Sometimes it was hard to keep track of who was who in my stories, but they tried their best! Tommy was a popular topic with us lately, and although they couldn't offer actual advice, it was helpful just to be able to have a friend say, "That is awesome" or "Man, that sucks."

    I had been seeing Tommy two or three times a week. He brought out a mellow side of me that was unfamiliar. Whether we were fucking, watching TV or lying on the beach I thoroughly enjoyed his company. Sometimes I stayed over consecutive nights because the time flew by so fast. I liked the fact that he had long-term Lifestyle relationships as well as vanilla and that he had experience as a single male. It made him more understanding of my situation. I was so satisfied that I hardly met any new people and I scarcely saw my other single guys. Some days I didn't even check my email. Although I was too smart to dive in head first with my eyes closed, I guess the hopeless romantic in me still felt the urge to dip my toe in the water.

This was unfamiliar territory for me because although I had totally wanted to date Peter, our relationship was never as deep or as public (in the vanilla world) as mine and Tommy's. Tommy was not Peter and I was not the same girl I was back then. Maybe this would turn out better. Who knew?

I accompanied Tommy to his cousin's wedding and was interrogated by strangers who assumed I was his girlfriend. When I said we weren't dating, they demanded to know why. Having to justify our situation but not being able to tell them the truth made me so uncomfortable. I was annoyed by their questions but also by the fact that part of me wished I could say I was his girlfriend. It would be so much easier. I was 100 percent happy with our arrangement, but once again, society was making me begin to feel awful. Tommy was very secure with himself and unfazed.

A few weeks later, we went to the nude beach because a group of his swinger friends were having their yearly reunion. The dynamic was much more social than intimate (as with Billy). I forced myself to appear calm and outgoing in this overwhelming group of high-energy people instead of quietly melting into the safety of Billy's undivided attention. I only had a portion of Tommy's because he was busy mingling with friends he hadn't seen in ages. It was totally understandable and acceptable, but being alone made me feel vulnerable. Our bonding was not the reason for my presence there. I wanted a glimpse into his life. I wanted to see what his version of socializing was. I wanted to witness his behavior among girls he had history with. When I saw people wearing t-shirts that read "Nude Lives Matter" and "Let's Make America Naked Again" I thought this would be easier to handle than the vanilla event. More acceptable since we were all swingers. No prying questions. But I was wrong. Vanilla or swinger, people had no filters when it came to being nosy.

Chapter 19. A Potential Peter

Tommy and I were clearly there together but no one knew our specific situation. I had several awkward encounters because I was still apprehensive about exactly how Tommy felt about me, so I was easily offended. A couple on the blanket next to us commented that Tommy was always showing up with random beautiful girls and I was the most recent. Why did they assume I would find that amusing? Why was I simply just another piece of ass? Why couldn't he in fact like me? Another older woman saw us sitting together, holding hands and kissing. She came over and said I was so much friendlier than his ex and he never smiled with her the way he smiled with me. She had a good feeling about me. What if I didn't want to be compared to his ex because I wasn't his girlfriend? Why couldn't people just let us be? A female acquaintance of his asked him to hang out sometime soon right in front of me. The body language clearly meant she was offering to fuck him. I was taken aback, thinking that was inappropriate. Why did she assume he was not exclusively with me? Why was she so sure he wanted to fuck her instead of me? Just because we were Lifestyle didn't mean you could do and say whatever you wanted. Tommy said she was new and probably didn't understand the etiquette.

As we were packing up our gear I ran into an unexpected person—Billy. I gave him a warm hug and introduced him to Tommy. After a few brief exchanges Billy waved good-bye and I said, "Talk to you soon." I wondered what Tommy thought. As he folded a towel, Tommy said, "I guess that was one of your playmates," and I casually said yes. Was it just an observation or was he jealous? What was Billy thinking? Was he surprised to see me with another guy or did he not care? Even though we were swingers, I still felt slightly uncomfortable. I didn't want one interfering with the other.

Tommy and I slowly made the long, sandy journey back to civilization. A short, stocky bald man with glasses and a long brown *Duck Dynasty*-type beard appeared on the left side of Tommy. Wearing khaki shorts, a white wife beater tank top and no shoes, and carrying one black sneaker in his right hand, he huffed and puffed as he tried to maintain a fast pace. I gave him a friendly smile and he saw this as an invitation to talk. He waved his lone shoe in the air and proclaimed he was having the worst luck. He and his wife met another couple on the beach who invited them to play. They had all headed back to the parking lot when he realized one of his shoes was missing. Defeated, he had to suffer the long, painful walk back to retrieve it and hoped his opportunity with the other couple wasn't ruined. Tommy and I looked at each other, confused, and simultaneously said, "Why the hell did you go back for the shoe?" "Fuck her barefoot," I suggested. "Buy a new shoe later," said Tommy. The man laughed. "After this hike I may not even have the energy to fuck her. I'm gonna need a nap." "I don't buy this charade," Tommy said sarcastically. "I think you purposely left your shoe behind so you had an excuse to not fuck her." The man joked back, "Yes, exactly. It was my plan all along to ditch them and find you two instead." The three of us enjoyed the witty banter all the way to the restroom facilities where we found his wife waiting for him. Our new friend introduced us to her, calling me by my name and referring to Tommy as my husband.

WTF? A hilarious interaction quickly turned sour. It was an innocent comment, but it enraged me. Why did everyone assume things? Why was I so sensitive? Probably the result of dating a married man for eight years. Being kept a secret and not having my feelings validated in public. Living in hiding. It was a sore spot, for sure. I never want to feel that way again.

I was starting to feel more like myself around Tommy and less like Scarlet. Our time together did not revolve around sex. We saw movies and went to the amusement park and pool halls. He appreciated both parts of my personality and respected my crabbish ways. He never pressured me when I momentarily retreated into my shell. But now, that accomplishment led to more anxiety—was he using me? I couldn't fully relax until we had a solid agreement. I was not jealous; I was insecure.

I didn't want to be traded in for the next girl after all the energy I had invested in him. I would prefer he didn't fuck other single girls behind my back, but I was not in a position to make demands. It would feel like cheating even though it most certainly wasn't. Logically I could separate things but emotionally it was difficult. I didn't know if he would be upset if I slept with another guy. Now I was getting nervous.

We discussed whether our situation was categorized as purely Lifestyle, friends with benefits or something more. We agreed it was on a questionable path where we didn't have a label but there were undeniable feelings. We both had a lot of baggage—my fear of commit-

Chapter 19. A Potential Peter 163

ment due to my exes and his recent heartbreak over a broken engagement. We didn't want to ruin what we had by rushing into a relationship too quickly, but the unknown was just as scary. Formally dating would create a new set of issues. Only time would tell, and we would cross that bridge when we came to it. Thinking about it gave me a migraine.

After a few more months, however, it was decision time. The warning signs were getting harder to ignore. I refused to have another Peter on my hands. I explained as nicely as I could that I was no longer comfortable filling the role of his fake girlfriend. We needed to agree whether we should become exclusive or tone things down. Giving so much energy to him meant I was missing out on the possibility of meeting someone who did want to date. I understood he was still coping with his breakup, but I was a believer in moving forward. Tommy told me he was too heartbroken, as if I didn't understand the concept. I assured him my heart was so mangled I was surprised I could even feel a connection anymore. I thought he was just blind. He could let his painful past keep him in a purgatory of wretchedness instead of choosing to move on and appreciate the opportunity in front of him to be happy. We were at a stalemate. Tommy was completely conflicted, so I chose to put a boundary back between us. I was going to be captain of the sinking ship. I would not be at his mercy. From then on, we would behave like regular casual partners. We promised to remain friends and I admit there was a brief adjustment. No more texting all day, no good night or good morning.

Once the dust settled, my vision was clearer. I focused on the differences we had and assured myself it would never have worked anyway. I mean, he had terrible taste in movies, which would drive me crazy. I am deeply moved by cinema and theater and music where he seemed disinterested. I love dancing and he refused even to try. I am animated, and my emotions are extremely lively, while his personality was neutral. I live in the moment and he had his retirement plans set in stone. I am a very thoughtful person and he was not very empathetic. The more I thought about it, the less compatible we were. He was obsessed with social media and texted while he drove which infuriated me. And most important, our sexual preferences were not the same beyond one on one. So, no—he was not my missing puzzle piece. Plus, I guess having a Rolodex of guys I could fill the void with helped. I was able to escape unscathed.

My first call was to Billy who always put a smile on my face. My second was to Luis to announce I was back in the market for something titillating. I had more than 200 unanswered emails representing potential replacements as well. There was always a "next."

Chapter 20

Out of My Shell

Whenever I told Lifestyle friends about my previous vanilla dating attempts, they laughed. They all had the same response: it would never work. You could take the girl out of the Lifestyle, but never the Lifestyle out of the girl. And, apparently, I was a true Lifestyle girl no matter how hard I tried to fight it. I guess I had just been too concerned with other people's opinions and how I was perceived.

The Lifestyle is just as it sounds—a style of living, not solely sex. It encompasses a set of beliefs and a way of thinking. If I could mix my two lives, then maybe I could finally be solid. Why couldn't I be both? I am Scarlet, and Scarlet is me. We are two halves that make one whole. There should be no distinction between a vanilla friend and a Lifestyle friend. They are all just my friends. And I am always me. What constitutes a friend, anyway? Someone who would drive you to the airport or help you move? Someone who knows your darkest secrets? Someone who remembers your birthday? Someone you have the most fun with? I spend most of my time with Lifestyle people. I have borrowed husbands for Broadway shows and Latin dancing. I have accompanied single guys to comedy clubs, aquariums, ice-skating rinks and haunted houses. On birthdays I get more wishes from vanilla friends but on holidays I receive more texts from Lifestyle friends.

I have accepted my "crab" persona. According to my research, hermit crabs also symbolize survival and resourcefulness since they must find a new shell each time they outgrow their current shell. Being attached to their shell means they are essentially always at home no matter where they end up. And, interestingly enough, hermit crabs are often labeled solitary creatures, but they actually crave social connections—just on their own terms. Maybe I was a hermit crab in a past life and not a mermaid. Many people only know me as "Shelly" and never know my real name.

I recently had another revelation about my baggage. I have fucked several hundred people since I have been on the site, yet I have never technically slept an entire night in a bed with any of them. I laid awake in bed while Max slept, cuddled with Billy and rubbed his hair while he napped, but I never relaxed enough to officially sleep. My friends made fun of me because it seemed to be such a strange boundary to have. I could fuck you, suck your dick, fuck your friends, and so on, but I couldn't sleep with you. I would tell them sleeping in a bed was too personal. Even as much in love with Peter as I was, I was notorious for sleeping on couches or sneaking out in the middle of the night. I even crawled out of bed and slept on the fucking floor like a dog!

Upon deeper reflection, I realized my issue was slightly more specific. I related sleeping to serious dating which I equated to possession. I could not separate current partners from the pain of past partners. Trying to sleep with someone was impossible. I panicked, my heart raced and I felt like I was going to suffocate. Being comfortable enough to sleep meant I was close enough to get hurt. I finally realized this was preventing me from receiving the full experience with the other person. I tried to embrace the fact he wanted to spend the night wrapped in my arms and appreciate the closeness. Sleeping did not need to represent anything other than sharing a bed. I was going to try to work on this. As silly as it sounds, I "practiced" sleeping in certain understanding male friends' beds. I stayed in bed a few minutes longer before escaping to the couch. If I got up to go to the bathroom in the middle of the night I crept back into bed for a few moments and laid next to my friend without waking him before returning to the couch. Baby steps. I did eventually conquer my fear and slept peacefully for a night beside several of them. Eventually I was able to spend the night with a few NSA dates. I was still selective who I slept next to, but when I made the effort, to be held all night was rewarding. Plus, I got to have the much-loved morning sex! It was a win-win.

I was raised to believe monogamy was the right way, the only way. But while most people are lucky to find one person who cares about them, I am fortunate to have several people who do at any given time. I have multiple relationships without the guilt of cheating or being dis-

Chapter 20. Out of My Shell

honest. I enjoy the benefits of great sex, affection and friendship without the headaches of arguing over typical things like paying bills or doing the dishes. We share the good and bad moments in our lives and are supportive without being committed. We see each other when we can with no pressure.

Maybe I never had a problem. Maybe I was just doing what I needed in *that* moment. Having fun. Exploring. Developing. Over the years, I have adjusted my swinging not because it was wrong but simply to fit my current needs since they are constantly evolving. Maybe I am so guarded and scarred from my previous relationships that I can't have a normal one right now. I am one of those animals in the TV commercial needing rescue with Sarah McLachlan singing in the background. So dejected and forsaken. Beaten down and abused by previous owners but still deserving love from someone. As much as I wanted closeness and security, maybe deep down I feared commitment because I associated it with control and loss of my freedom.

Swinging allows me both sides. What I yearned for last week I may hate this week. I am free to be as active or wild as I want or go dormant. I can switch from multiple guys to just one and I don't need to justify why. I can be cold and unattached or affectionate and intimate. I can have a clean break. Maybe I do not need to be ashamed because I have found a place where I fit in. Instead of feeling alone for having this secret I can be grateful to have access to a site where tens of thousands of other people have the same desires. I am not alone. This lifestyle accepts me. It is all about me—what I want, how, when, where, but not why. I have finally realized the why does not matter and that is a beautiful and powerful thing.

Writing this book has been immensely therapeutic. With the help of my coach, I have concluded that I have everything I thought I was missing. It is just packaged in an unusual way and has a unique label. This life works for me—at least right now. I have no idea what the future holds and that is fine. I will no longer try to force a life I do not believe in. I will never stop dreaming of finding my swinger Prince Charming to fall in love with and live happily ever after as a Lifestyle power couple. Right now, my love life stands at a seven.

Chapter 21

Red Hot

Time to let Scarlet out.

Now that my emotions were contained, my focus shifted back to fucking other people. I was ready to dive back in with a vengeance—no holds barred. I was going to get out of my comfort zone and push whatever limits remained. Thrive in the chaos of this never-ending carousel of carnal pleasure and potential lovers. Be myself and not overthink every little thing.

September (My First Self-Orchestrated MFM)

Lenny and Charlie had both texted me to make plans. I got daring and asked if they would be up for a threesome. Couldn't hurt, I thought. To my surprise, they agreed with no hesitation. My bravery paid off!

I met Charlie at the hotel around 8 p.m. We were already fucking when there was a knock on the door around 9:30. I dismounted Charlie and answered the door naked and flushed. Lenny walked in and kissed me hello. I quickly introduced the fellas and resumed fucking Charlie, but with him on top. Lenny got undressed immediately and put his hard cock in my mouth. After a few minutes, he politely asked Charlie if he could take a turn. Charlie said, "Sure" and they switched positions. Lenny fucked me until he came then passed me back to Charlie. I was riding Charlie when Lenny rejoined from behind. "You two okay with DV?" I asked, casually. Both nodded yes. Such easy-going fellas. DV was fun but brief as Charlie came. "Lenny, I'm out," he said. "She's all yours." Lenny flipped me onto my back and gladly took over. Charlie returned and I sucked his cock as Lenny fucked me in the ass. He shouted how good and tight I was and Charlie needed to try this next. Lenny came and Charlie fucked me. They were a terrific tag team. Especially for total strangers. Charlie fucked me in the ass and I was surprised that I was so into it. Normally I wasn't that free with anal, but I was so turned on I went with it.

I heard the water turn on in the shower and Lenny got cleaned up. Charlie was still performing strong. I noticed Lenny getting dressed out of the corner of my eye. "Hey, where are you going?" He apologetically said he needed to go to work. "So, you drove two hours just to fuck me for a half hour? That is insane." "I know but I couldn't turn you down," Lenny replied. "Your pussy is too good." That was super flattering. I kissed him good-bye and he thanked Charlie for sharing.

Charlie and I fucked awhile longer before he came all over my face. Again, I was in an exceptionally wild mood, so nothing seemed to bother me. We watched TV then fucked again. I left around 2 a.m. feeling invigorated.

October (Fantastic Foursome)

This was a big night and very out of character for me. A foursome with Tommy (whom I had not seen since our fake breakup) and Luis and his wife Elena (whom I have only ever seen in vanilla situations). The three of them had played together many times so we seemed a natural fit. I debated canceling but the plans were made prior to my downfall with Tommy and I hadn't had a foursome in ages. I was curious to interact with Elena in a sexual environment. I had never fucked Luis in front of her. How would that be? Would we use condoms or all fuck raw? Would we be in separate beds or all together? Would she interact with me? So many questions filled my mind.

I arrived at Tommy's at 7:30 p.m. It was a little awkward as I wasn't sure how to behave. I prayed Luis and Elena would get there soon—I needed a buffer. The conversation with Tommy seemed forced and there was some tension. I showered to escape the uncomfortableness.

At 8:15, the door opened, and Luis and Elena descended the stairs with big smiles. She kissed Tommy hello and then attacked me with a mammoth hug so forceful we toppled over onto the bed. I was surprised she was so happy to see me. It was very sweet. The four of us sat around and talked, catching up. I kept wondering how and when our play would start.

Eventually Luis stood up and approached me from behind. He wrapped his arms around me and grunted. I said, "Oh boy" because I knew the beast was awake. Tommy replied, "Here we go" and lowered the lights. Luis pushed me toward the bed and pulled my pants down. I glanced over and saw Tommy and Elena were already naked and kissing. I was on my back and Luis was fucking me when Tommy and Elena joined us on the large bed. Elena and I remained next to each other as the boys fucked us and went down on us, made us squirt.

Occasionally, Luis would call "Switch!" and they would switch. Elena and I lightly touched each other's bodies, held hands for solidarity. Squeezed each other's hands as we came. We kissed as they fucked us. Her mouth was so soft. We had good chemistry. We all fucked in every position and scenario possible.

It was total porn style. The craziest part was when Luis sat on the couch and I knelt on the floor and sucked his cock. Elena stood behind me and bent over, putting her stomach on my back. Tommy took turns fucking each of us, back and forth. Elena sucked Luis's dick as I licked his balls. This was teamwork at its finest, for sure! The four of us were so compatible. Everything flowed perfectly and naturally.

The guys DVed me, which Elena passed on. She bowed out first and fell asleep on the couch as the guys took turns with me. Around midnight we called it quits. We had to work the next day. The three of them unanimously voted this the best foursome they ever had. It was phenomenal, they agreed. I was pleased to be the missing piece they had been seeking for so long.

Luis, Elena and I bid farewell to Tommy and headed to the diner. We were starving!

Luis went to the ATM across the street, so Elena and I had alone time. We chatted like regular gal pals. Elena ordered a turkey and cheese club with sweet potato fries for Luis. He always ate the same thing. I interjected, "Don't forget his honey mustard," and Elena nodded. "Good call." It was a strange dynamic. The wife and the side piece bonding over ordering his meal. Not weird in the slightest. Priceless, I thought. I truly loved this couple.

Chapter 21. Red Hot

November (Gang Life)

Over the course of my long career swinging, one milestone eluded my portfolio—the infamous gang bang. I never thought of myself as a gang bang candidate even with all my previous antics, but I was an ambitious girl. I called Luis to announce I was ready.

In preparation for my big night, I had not had sex in two days and skipped the gym. I didn't have any details about what the night would involve but I knew I needed to conserve my energy. Planning a group event was not an easy task. Luis spent countless hours searching for the perfect guys which, from experience, I knew was a tedious process, so I brought him his favorite carrot cake from my old bakery as a token of my gratitude. I met Luis at 8 p.m. and he drove us to an undisclosed location. I was completely serene and didn't ask any questions. I was filled with curiosity and excitement as if I was going to a surprise party I accidentally found out someone was throwing for me. I just went along for the ride.

We arrived at a house and Luis let us in through an open door. "Where is everyone?" "They will be here soon. Just get changed." I traded my t-shirt and jeans for a sheer white outfit that consisted of thin horizontal strips of fabric leaving most of my skin exposed. Luis had bought it for me when we first met, and it was my favorite lingerie. I wandered around the empty rooms beginning to get butterflies. I was so amped. I was ready. Luis called me into the bedroom where he had set up a cooler full of drinks for the guests and a Bluetooth speaker streamed a personalized playlist for me. He kissed me softly. "Let me see that pussy." "Now?" I asked with a hint of confusion. "You never touch me first. You always wait 'til the end." "I want you now. Yes, let's get you warmed up." I willingly laid on the bed and he slipped my panties off and stuffed his cock inside me, alternating between my pussy and ass. "Oh, you are going to be a good little anal girl tonight. I can tell." "We shall see," I chuckled. "Well, you should at least let the host fuck you in the ass." "Perhaps."

We fucked for close to half an hour before the guests began trickling in and one by one joined the rotation. Eventually it was five against one—three black guys, one Spanish and Luis—my first gang bang. A gang bang was a unique situation for me because it went against my normal protocols. This night primarily focused on hardcore fucking and stamina without an introduction, chemistry, or sensual connection. I never would have chosen any of these guys, but Luis was my anchor providing the intimacy and security and they were literally just functional equipment. "What is your safe word?" one asked. "Banana, but just so you know, I have only used it once the entire time I have known Luis," I taunted. "Be careful," Luis interjected. "She knows how to play possum. Don't let her fool you." That was the beginning of the battle of wills. These guys wanted to destroy me, and I wanted to prove they couldn't. No one wanted to surrender to anyone. I was impressed with the skill and determination these guys brought. They folded my body into positions I never imagined—thank God I did yoga for so many years! Their BBCs (big black cocks) reached so deep inside me I could feel them in my stomach. We ran a DV train—Luis stayed on the bottom with me on top and the other guys took turns offering the second cock. Each duo felt completely different.

I was in the boxing ring and Luis was my manager. My body was getting attacked and my mental game had to be just as strong as my physical game. In between rounds, Luis gave me water and told me to walk around and stretch my muscles. "You are strong. Show these boys who is the boss." "I am so proud of you," he would cheer. The match lasted just over three hours and I proved I was worthy of my reputation. The guys were shocked at my endurance and one said, "I have never met a girl who didn't use her safe word with me." Luis said, "I warned you about her. I only bring the best." All the participants agreed I was stellar and hoped to have the chance to cross my path again. I felt victorious.

At the diner, I was starving but could barely eat. Ironically, my pussy was totally fine from all the fucking, but my stomach was a mess from flexing my ab muscles to brace for impact all night.

Luis and I compared notes about the night—we rated the night at an 80 percent because out of five guys the Spanish one was not up to par. That was a pretty good score! Neither of us would have sex for the next few days—it would be sacrilegious to try and follow that phenomenal night with anything else, like eating a filet mignon at a five-star restaurant and eating a Big Mac at McDonald's the next day. It tainted the experience. Instead, you needed to savor the moment and reflect on it. "I was surprised you spent so much time on your back. I know you love to be on top usually." Very observant. I raised an eyebrow. "1. I had nothing to prove. I wanted them to do the work. 2. I needed to pace myself. It was not easy for my body to sustain that much abuse." "Good girl. You are getting very smart." "I told you—*Shelly is back.*"

December

Luis and I celebrated our one-year anniversary with a special evening. I bought a skimpy little black dress and actually wore high heels. We dined at an Italian restaurant attached to the hotel where we planned to stay. We reminisced about the first time we met and the past 12 months. The conversation was lovely and the food was delicious. At 9 he checked his watch and said, "Gotta get upstairs." I knew better than to ask any questions. Whatever he had planned I was up for. "Damn, I forgot the blindfold," he said. "No problem," I replied, handing him the extra red linen napkin on our table. He winked.

In the elevator Luis told me to be a good girl and informed me I had the freedom to do what I wanted. He was providing the actors, but I was directing the movie.

Once we were in the room, Luis gave me a bottle of expensive perfume. How thoughtful. Then he handed me a new lacy red outfit. I unzipped my dress and changed into the lingerie. We laughed as he tied the napkin around my eyes. I sat on the bed and waited for a knock on the door. Guys arrived every ten or 15 minutes until we had six in the room.

Although I had permission to remove the blindfold, I chose to keep it on. It allowed me to focus on feeling and not thinking. The guys assumed I was submissive and spoke to Luis instead of me. "Tell her yourself," he would say. "She's the boss. Don't let her fool you." I recognized the voices of two of the guys from previous gatherings; the others were unfamiliar.

For several hours my six new friends and I played. Unlike the previous gang bang, these guys were instructed to be rough but sensual. The entire vibe was sexier. I was a spoiled princess instead of an object. It was glorious. I loved trying to guess who was doing what to me, who

I was kissing and so on. They took turns performing DV with alternating partners.

Around midnight they began leaving one at a time. They would lean over and kiss me good-bye and tell me it had been a pleasure meeting me. I heard them thank Luis for the invite.

The remaining guy was someone I knew so I finally discarded the blindfold. Makeup was smeared across my face. "Whew!" I exclaimed. "That was crazy!" With my vision restored I properly said hello to him. We fucked a little while longer then relaxed and chatted before he left.

With the party over, I crawled into bed with Luis. We had sex and then fell asleep. It was one of my favorite nights. I guess I am a gang bang girl.

December 31

I felt blessed to spend New Year's with people who cared about me. Along with a few other Lifestyle friends, including Tommy, I spent the evening at Luis's house. I brought small gifts for his wife and kids. Luis gave me a jewelry box and inside was an ankle bracelet with a decorative seashell on it. We ate dinner, played board games and drank champagne at midnight. No sexual activity occurred. We were just a group of friends. I was where I belonged. This was the epitome of the Lifestyle for me—finally.

Epilogue

My life is wonderful. My social life is thriving, both vanilla and Lifestyle. I have several freelance jobs, which afford me a flexible schedule and little stress, and I have enrolled in online classes to finish my college degree. I have recently traveled to Europe and the Caribbean. Oh, and let's not forget, *my book is being published!*

Unfortunately, Tommy faded away without any explanation. I think he was a victim of "The grass is always greener on the other side" syndrome. Thanks to my experience with Peter, I accepted guys like Tommy were just temporary sources of companionship and date nights. Don't get me wrong, I sulked for a few days, but I didn't suffer when he abruptly disappeared because I finally understood these relationships were not meant to last forever. The fact that I never even considered contacting him spoke volumes about my personal progress. His loss. I was able to let go. People are simply there one day, gone the next. When one door closes, another opens. I found a handful of new partners whose longevity was unknown but were making me smile for the time being.

A few rockstar guys miraculously stood the test of time! Luis and I are still great friends (just over a year). He provides most of my audacious adventures one day and I am joining his family on a fun outing to the zoo or the circus the next day. Billy (two years) remains a good friend whom I see when our schedules allow, and he always makes me feel like a million bucks. Max (almost three years) and I keep in touch and I call him when I need to confide in someone. Whether it's the guys I have already met or the countless guys I may meet in the future—I value the time we spend together and feel truly grateful to share my life with them.

Extra Info

My Swinger Profiles

Original

Single female—used to be a couple now playing alone.
Looking for ongoing encounters with guys who are genuine and respectful.
Please be in good shape.
No smokers.
Local is ideal.
Have been to clubs but prefer meeting privately.
Open to meeting couples, bi curious.
Please open face pics when contacting me.
Don't be shy—say hello!

Next

Guide to catching a Unicorn!
* Unicorns are scared of the unknown—must see face pics immediately, credits preferred
* Unicorns cannot cross bridges or they die—you must travel to me
* Unicorns like athletic bodies—please know what a gym is
* Unicorns do not appreciate vulgar or disrespectful emails—it makes them sad
* Unicorns don't like jealousy—it frightens them
* Unicorns are classy and never share X-rated pictures—so do not ask

* Unicorns don't have a lot of free time—don't waste it, be reliable

* Unicorns are allergic to latex—please be prepared

Current

Looking For:

STOP WASTING MY TIME. There are a lot of options on here so if you piss me off or act like a jerk you will be immediately forgotten and replaced. No wonder single guys get a bad reputation. So many assholes.

** I am not here to help you cheat on your girlfriend/wife

** If you are not prepared to travel to a hotel near me; do not bother contacting me

** If I say no, stop asking. It will always be no

** If you think "wanna fuck?" is a good opening sentence, I am not for you

** If you don't have phenomenal stamina, keep moving—this is not amateur hour

** Squirt-inducing skills are not required, but definitely preferred

** If you can't hold a normal conversation, you will never keep my attention

** Funny guys get bonus points

** If you think you are doing me a favor by fucking me, you are wrong. I have an unlimited supply of willing candidates

** Free members with no pics and no credits = NO chance. Leave me alone

** Catch my interest—be unique

** Straight single males with very fit bodies only.

I MUST SEE FACE PICS.

I prefer experienced gentlemen who are accredited, under 45

Please be reliable and respectful

I like passionate sex and guys with good stamina

I like to be sweaty and out of breath—the sheets should be soaked!

I am very turned on by a good kisser

Open to a LTR with the right guy

I am 100 percent real

Extra Info 179

I love MFM, MFMM, MFMMM (straight guys) if you have a hot friend let me know :)

ALLERGIC TO LATEX, please have proper condoms, Skyn is a good brand

I am mostly straight but bi friendly—open to couples with credits and face pics—must be attracted to both of you and there needs to be zero jealousy/rules

A Sexual Girl Scout

Swingers are practical regarding sex and I learned to always be prepared. Sex could present itself at any moment, when you least expected it. You could get an email from a new person or a spontaneous invite from a past playmate. You just never knew.

- Always be waxed. I was on a strict three-week schedule.
- Carry your own condoms, regular and Magnum—something for everyone. This was important for me as I am allergic to latex.
- Keep a pair of sexy underwear, Summer's Eve wipes and a travel toothbrush in your purse.
- Always turn on the A/C or position a fan for proper air circulation. Even if the space seems too cold, it will get hot.
- Don't wear mascara. I looked like a raccoon after a few rounds of sweaty sex.
- Stock up on water and Gatorade—insane sex is a good way to get dehydrated fast. Funny but true.
- Keep lube in easily accessible spots and be aware of outlet locations, making sure they are close enough to the bed or have an extension cord nearby to ensure toys can be plugged in.
- Spread towels or old blankets over the bed to absorb sweat, semen and other fluids. You can remove them and have a clean area for sleeping.
- When playing in a group, tie your underwear around your wrist so you don't lose them. This was one of the best tips I ever learned! I lost many pairs of underwear before a friend (a male friend, ironically) told me this trick.

The Anonymous Letter a Neighbor Sent Me

I must honestly say I feel very odd composing this letter to you, but the problem I am going to tell you about has continued for several months and is now not only affecting my sleep, but my job performance as well. It is about your sex. The walls are paper thin. I can hear you moaning when I'm in my living room, but I ignore it since I'm awake.

HOWEVER, when it is after 10PM and I'm trying to sleep on the week night I am being kept awake. Look, I'm not asking you to stop your sex life on my account, but I'm wondering if you could be more considerate. I know … an odd request, but maybe you could start earlier so it doesn't go on past 10PM or maybe you could have sex in the living room. There is a city noise ordinance on the week nights at 9PM. To be honest, the noise coming from your bedroom is LOUD. Yes, I've had neighbors before you living there that engaged in sexual activity, but like I said the walls are thin and the noise coming from your place is VERY LOUD.

I felt it was better I wrote you rather than banging on the walls, ceiling or floor to insinuate the disturbance.

Thank you and I appreciate your consideration.

Crazy but True

Once I met a guy who promised me via text the craziest, wildest sex I could imagine. He drove two hours and showed up with a broken arm! Yep, he wore a cast from his elbow to his wrist. Now, the situation with Tommy's broken arm was different—we were friends and we knew what we were attempting. Plus, Luis was there to help. This was a total blind-side. And, if you ask me, inappropriate for a first time.

I asked why he didn't cancel the date or at least postpone. He bragged about how much pleasure he could provide using just one hand. He was an expert with the ladies. He wasn't concerned at all. He kept ogling me in a creepy way. I knew he was full of shit and I hated arrogant men. Just to humor him, I agreed to go to the hotel. I was going to offer no assistance. I knew there would be no sex; I just wanted to see how committed he was to this farce.

He could barely get the condom on with one hand. It took forever. I just sat back and watched him struggle. Finally, he was ready to go but he couldn't figure out what position was best because his balance was off. I sensed having two working hands would not make him much more skilled. I yawned. I was so *not* turned on. How long until he admitted he was not capable? Suddenly he requested I get on top because that would solve all the problems. I laughed as I declined. "Give me a break," he pleaded. "I'm injured." What happened to the macho man? I got dressed and wished him a lovely evening as I sauntered out the door. We were in the hotel less than 20 minutes.

Some people may think that was cruel of me. But again, I stand by the fact that a lot of guys try to take advantage of girls. Sometimes they need to be humbled so the next girl can be treated better.

Being a Cougar

It was brought to my attention that I was old enough to be a cougar. I didn't feel old! WTF? But when I was 32, I was told fucking a 21-year-old qualified me as one. I had always gravitated toward older men, so I investigated a few younger men but never got much out of them sexually. They were so innocent and inexperienced. They couldn't afford hotel rooms. They didn't know how to handle an aggressive, experienced woman like me. They were apprehensive and came too fast. My favorite story was when one of them claimed to be at basketball practice. He had to leave right after the sex because his mom was making his favorite meal, chicken cutlets. Dinner was served at 8 o'clock sharp and he couldn't be late. I almost died laughing.

I was their "older woman" fantasy. They would never forget me, but I could barely remember the differences between them. It was another check on the bucket list.

Cell Phone Betrayal

Since my phone was filled with X-rated pictures and dirty text messages, I guarded it with my life. I never left it unattended or let anyone borrow it, and I always had the auto lock engaged. If I wanted to share a cool photo with someone I would text it to them, so they could not accidentally touch a button or swipe the wrong way and inadvertently reveal my dark secrets. When texting, I always triple checked recipients before hitting send. Didn't want to send a vanilla person a Lifestyle message by mistake. When I read an incoming text, I always covered the screen with my hand, so a surprise dick pic would not create an awkward moment. In one instance, though, I was unexpectedly screwed.

I leased a new car and the sales guy, a young Jamaican kid in his early 20s, offered to help me get familiarized with the fancy new settings. I sat in the driver's seat as he gave me the overview from the passenger's seat. He programmed my favorite radio stations and explained how to use the navigation system through my cell phone. I was very distracted by the excitement of my new SUV, so when he asked if I wanted him to sync the Bluetooth feature, I absentmindedly nodded yes. It seemed harmless at first until I realized all my contacts were being loaded onto the small touch screen my sales guy was staring directly at.

They popped up one at a time, in alphabetical order. Aunt Julie, Aunt Carolyn.... I started to sweat as my brain frantically scrolled through my Rolodex, which included 20 percent vanilla friends, family and coworkers and 80 percent swingers. To keep track of all my Lifestyle associates I always entered them as their first name plus their screen names from the sex site. Most screen names included various profane and graphic words. As and Bs were safe, but I knew for a fact Cs were going to become a problem, a very embarrassing one. Carol—insurance agent, Chris—hotwifefucker, Chad—pussyeater2016, Dad, Dad cell, Danny—hardcock4u33, Dentist—Dr. Anderson, Dom—analluver825. I tried to divert his attention by inquiring about gas mileage. I prayed for him to look anywhere except that damn screen. Greg—cuminyourmouth00. Henry—gangbangpro. Can this get any worse, I thought? Yes, it could. Couples began sporadically appearing in between.... Mary & Brian—weluv2fuk, Mom, Mom cell. Why is the fucking alphabet so long? We both acted like nothing inappropriate was happening. He stuttered as he asked if he gave me my spare set of keys. Ten minutes felt like ten hours as my extensive phone book finally synced. My throat was parched. I was in dire need of a sip of water. Or a shot of something stronger.

Extra Info

Abbreviations and Terms

BBC: big black cock
BI: you have sex with guys and girls
BULL: a dominant male who cuckolds wives
CUCKOLD: a sexually inadequate husband who accepts his wife's pussy is her property and she decides who she will fuck even if it means denying her husband
D&D: drug and disease free, clean
DP: double penetration of penises (anal and vaginal at once)
DV: double vaginal (two penises at once)
EXHIBITIONIST: likes to be watched, gets turned on by it
F: female
FMF: threesome with two females and one male
FULL SWAP: changing partners for intercourse
FWB: friends with benefits (a step above NSA)
GANG BANG: one woman getting fucked by several men
HOST: can entertain/provide a place to play
HOT WIFE: happily married woman who has her husband's blessing to fuck other guys
LS: lifestyle
LTR: long-term relationship (very rare to see that, but it is in my profile)
M: male
MF: male and female couple
MFM: threesome with two straight males and one female
MFMM: one woman with three men
MFMMM: one woman with four men
MMF: threesome with two bi males and one female
NEWBIE: someone new/inexperienced
NSA: no strings attached
OFF SITE: no sex allowed
ON SITE: sex allowed
SEASONED: experienced
SOFT SWAP: changing partners for oral or other play, but no intercourse
UNICORN: single female
VANILLA: non-swinger
VOYEUR: likes to watch, gets turned on by it

www.ingramcontent.com/pod-product-compliance
Ingram Content Group UK Ltd.
Pitfield, Milton Keynes, MK11 3LW, UK
UKHW042014140426
5217IPUK00015B/1159